MAY YOU

*Experience Freedom from Your Past, Peace in
Your Present, and Hope for Your Future*

Jason Glaze

MAY YOU

*Experience Freedom from Your Past, Peace in
Your Present, and Hope for Your Future*

Jason Glaze

*May you be strengthened with all power, according to his glorious
might, for all endurance and patience with joy.*

—The Apostle Paul, Colossians 1:11

New Name Ministries, Dawsonville, GA

May You: Experience Freedom from Your Past, Peace in Your
Present, and Hope for Your Future.

Edited by Laura Button Woznick
Cover and Interior Design by Pat Malone
Printed by New London Press, Alpharetta, GA

ISBN-13: 978-0-9978318-0-1

DEDICATION

This book is dedicated to my parents, Doug and Joan Glaze.

The Oxford Universal Dictionary* defines a supporter as "One who sides with, backs up, assists, or countenances a person or cause."

Mom and Dad, your faithful support has created the foundation and paved the way for this work to flourish. I am forever grateful for all you've made possible. I love you both.

Your Son,

Jason

(Third edition, 1955)

CONTENTS

Author's Notes

My own spiritual journey is riddled with twists and turns. 2003 marked one of the more significant junctions. It was a year when I experienced God in a fresh way, my true self for the first time, and a new way to live. Through discipleship counseling and training, I experienced healing from several parts of my past that kept showing up in my present, and I received revelations that gave me a sense of freedom I had been craving.

To say my life has been filled with ups and downs, successes and failures since that turning point would be an understatement. During one season of my life, blinded by the darkness I created with my own sin, I began to doubt everything I thought to be true. I knew I needed to embrace my doubt because it was the only way to discover what was real.

The subjects I have chosen for this book are the ones that made it through the darkness and survived the fire of doubt. Giving them my deliberate and careful attention is essential to my relationships with God, myself, and others. They are a point of connection between my soul and health and have become a way for the Holy Spirit to keep His finger on my spiritual pulse.

Jason Glaze

About This Book
and How to Use It

May You was originally envisioned as an aid between counselors and counselees at New Name Ministries in Dawsonville, GA (newname.cc). If you are reading this book on your own or as part of a small group, we pray it will serve as an introduction to these topics and a springboard for you to learn and experience more. This book contains heavy subject matter, and you may find you need a trusted friend or mentor to walk with you through some or all of the topics. Additionally, you should seek individual counseling if needed. Please do not hesitate to seek someone out. We are not designed to journey alone.

At the end of each chapter, you will find the following sections:

1. A prayer for you to meditate on and to help you communicate with God.

2. Journal questions designed to help make the content personal for you. You will need to set aside a journal or notebook for use with this book.

3. Additional exercises to take you deeper into each subject. Be aware that you may not be ready to do all of these additional exercises immediately after you read the chapter. Make yourself a note and be intentional about returning to the exercises when the time is right.

As you read through the chapters, and especially as you work through the material at the end of each one, create the environment you need in order to be fully present to the Holy Spirit. Find a quiet place and remove any and all distractions. We are well aware that in this busy world, carving out quiet time is easier said than done, but you are worth it.

———

All Bible verses are quoted from the English Standard Version (ESV).

———

While I am the primary author of this text, I use the term "we" throughout as an acknowledgment that I am speaking for and distilling the experiences of the New Name Ministries Staff, myself, and many others who have found healing through the process outlined in this book.

Jason Glaze

INTRODUCTION
And So It Begins...

The term life change is not simply a meaningless cliché but a reality to be experienced. We know because we ourselves have experienced this reality. Our lives have been and are still being radically changed by God using the essentials of healing and growth found in this book. We pray God uses this book as an instrument of love to facilitate healing and as a bridge of hope leading you from mere knowledge about life to experiencing The Life.

You have probably opened this book because you are faced with a common problem. You have been fighting inward battles and, while you may have found temporary relief in the past, eventually find yourself tripping over the same stumbling blocks as before. Your current mental and emotional states are not what you want to be experiencing. You want change but don't know where to start or how to find it. You want to be comfortable in your own skin, but fear, shame, confusion, counterproductive behaviors, and broken or strained relationships leave you feeling trapped instead. You cannot think your way out of these problems. If you knew how to fix your life, you would have done it already.

No matter how long you've been struggling, there is hope. There is a knowledge above your own, a light that drives out the darkness, and a love that swallows up fear. Healing from whatever is creating your cycles of frustration is available. You can be free from your past, find peace in your present, and embrace a hope-filled future. The best part of this process is that you don't have to take the lead. God is in your past as you revisit it. He is the peace you need in your present to go on this journey. And He is already in your future as you discover the desires of your heart.

Where to start? To begin any healing process, an attitude of surrender is required. We must be willing to let go of our own efforts, plans, and agendas and surrender to the love of God if we want to experience healing and growth. He is aware of everything we need in detail. He knows the wounded, frightened, and numb areas of our souls. He is the Wonderful Counselor (Isaiah 9:6) who can be trusted to always have our best interests in His heart.

As you venture through these chapters, begin listening to the thoughts offered to you by Him instead of thinking your way through the process. Thinking your own thoughts is vastly different from listening to the thoughts that come from Him. Being willing to cooperate with the voice of Love and surrender to His lead are essential to this process. Your responsibility is your response to His ability.

As you begin to engage God with each of these subjects, be intentional; at the same time, be cautious about getting into a hurry when it comes to how fast you want to heal. While the chapters do build on each other, you should give each chapter its own attention rather than attempting to read through the entire book in one sitting. Follow the advice of the classical adage to "make haste slowly." Start today with an urgent patience, and be eager to dive in but swim calmly and deliberately.

On this journey, you will have the opportunity to discover and embrace your God-given needs. Then you will be invited to take a deep look at your own story to uncover wounds you have experienced and the beliefs stemming from those hurts. You will be challenged to see the futility of trying to make expectations work for you and the freedom of living from a new mindset. You will learn about your false self and how you have been functioning from it rather than from your true self. You will also be faced with owning the reality that your outward circumstances are not the cause of your problems. You will see the beauty of brokenness in a way that will cause you to crave it instead of avoid it.

Next, you will enter into the sacred endeavor of exploring your Concept of God, first having your eyes opened to who you thought He was, then allowing Jesus to show you the true character of His Father. You will be given the opportunity to leave your shame where God left it, on the cross. As your true identity is revealed, you will begin to realize you're not who you thought you were. Then you will have the courage to look at what it means to completely forgive.

You will find relief from the games your mind plays as you realize the destruction caused by living with judgments and vows. You will see grieving as a gift to be embraced instead of a consequence to be avoided. Love will quiet your fears and draw you into a life of surrender, freeing you from the agony of control.

We believe these are the most important areas of your soul to explore, the subjects that matter the most. Our goal is to cut through the fluff and talk about the essentials of healing and growing.

As you allow the messages in this book to challenge and change you, you may wonder why you waited so long to address these issues. Don't allow yourself to be sidetracked by regret. Keep in mind the Chinese proverb: "The best time to plant a tree was twenty years ago. The second best time is now."

Chapter One

Needs

All You Need Is Love

LOVE IS THE MOST ALLURING and powerful force in the universe. People die for it and kill for it. Battles have been fought over love, yet it has been the motivation behind great movements of peace. It has the power to rip our hearts to shreds one day and heal us the next. We are prone to take the necessities of physical life, such as air, light, food, and water, for granted. We do the same with our souls. If we understood that without love our souls would wither away to dust, we would value it more. Sadly, most people are attempting to live with dehydrated souls when relief is always available.

While each of us may describe the fruits of love with many different words, they all stem from the root of love. Some of the most commonly used words are:

worth	acceptance	security	respect
purpose	belonging	value	safety
nurturing	significance	intimacy	approval
cherishing	adoration	support	encouragement

Regardless of the different terms we may use to describe our emotional need, they all point back to the foundational need to feel loved.

Love is not merely a human desire, but a necessity, as shown by the way we live our lives. A person dying of thirst will go to any lengths required to get their need for water met. Similarly, our need for love influences our attitude and motivates our behavior. Until we experience getting this need met by the One who created it within us, we spend the majority of our time and energy striving to meet our need for love through our own strength and resources.

We begin developing our unique methods of finding love at a very young age and intuitively perfect our craft as the years go by. As we search for love, our natural instincts drive us to sources other than God. We often look to others, such as spouses, friends, or even our children, to make us feel loved. Other times, we try to find love in what we do or possess. We gain, acquire, achieve, and perform, constantly raising the bar, which leaves us feeling exhausted. Through this process, we complicate our lives and the lives of others by seeking to fill the void created by our unmet need.

Inevitably, seeking to meet our need for love in our own ways brings frustration. Our expectations frequently go unmet, creating anger and bitterness. We pump the wrong well until it is dry and then get angry at the well for running out of water. Our fear of being thirsty causes us to attempt to control, and after we've exhausted all our resources, creating pain for ourselves and others, we experience brokenness. At this point, we desire change, so we begin to entertain the thought that there is another way to live.

While recognizing our need for change can be difficult, those who are not intimately in touch with their need for love can find healing even more elusive. Certain personalities, depending on their past experiences, can develop an attitude that says, "I don't need love." If we have a hard time recognizing our need for love, it may be because our experiences of love have been few and far between or because we have a twisted view of what love looks like. If this describes you, allow your guard to drop, quiet your mind, and begin to sense that even though you have yet to discover your need for love, the Source of love has already discovered you.

It is a divine love story. God so longs for relationship with humanity that He created us to be incomplete without it. He wants a true, unconditional bond with us; therefore, we are given freedom to choose. He desires for us to find love in our relationship with Him, while giving us the choice to exhaust all other resources as we endlessly strive to fulfill our own need. This search becomes less complicated and exhausting as we realize we have been created with a built-in radar continually pointing us in His direction, and His love is a constant beacon drawing us back to Him.

WE PUMP THE WRONG WELL UNTIL IT IS DRY AND THEN GET ANGRY AT THE WELL FOR RUNNING OUT OF WATER.

While God desires for us to make Him the source that fulfills our emotional need for love, He does not want us to isolate ourselves from others. We will find ourselves feeling a tremendous deficit if we resist authentic relationship with other people. Our original design is to be in relationship with God, and from that relationship, love, value, respect, and honor others. Unless we genuinely connect with at least a few people, we will not be experiencing the richness of God's design for our lives.

Other people can be a pipeline to God's love, but we should never attempt to make each other the source to meet our emotional needs. We can know when we've attempted to treat others as our source by paying attention to our expectations. When we look to anyone other than God to meet our need for love, we place expectations on them to do what we think will make us feel the emotion we're searching for.

GOD IS THE PROVIDER OF EVERYTHING WE NEED FOR LIFE AND LOVE.

In our childhood, we begin developing methods and systems to attempt to fill our emotional cups. As years go by, we subconsciously perfect our craft and increase our frustrations. Thankfully, God's patient love is ever present as we journey from mirage to mirage, finally realizing the futility of trying to find love our way. As our relationship with God develops, we find He truly lives up to the name He has given Himself: I AM (Exodus 3:14). God is the provider of everything we need for life and love.

May you welcome your God-given need for love, and may that need guide you to its Source.

Prayer

Father, You have created me with a deep need for love, which means You have created me with a deep need for You. As I embrace my neediness, clearly convince me that You and You alone can meet my need for love. Teach me to freely receive love from You through whatever avenues You so choose. I open myself up and allow Your heart to touch mine. Amen.

In Your Journal...

1. What words other than love would you use to describe your emotional need? Some of the most common ones are worth, acceptance, security, respect, purpose, belonging, value, safety, nurturing, significance, intimacy, approval, cherishing, adoration, support, and encouragement, but feel free to use other words as well.

2. Other than God, whom or what have you looked to in the past as a source to meet your emotional needs? What about in the present? How has this worked for you?

3. Read the following sentence aloud several times: "Ultimately, only God can meet my emotional need for love." What are your honest thoughts and emotions concerning this statement?

FURTHER EXERCISES

———

Complete the following sentences in your journal.

1. I am most aware of my emotional need when...

2. I am least aware of my emotional need when...

3. The one thing that frightens me most about having an emotional need is...

4. Sometimes I wish I didn't have an emotional need because...

5. When I focus on others as a source to meet my emotional need, I feel...

6. When other people look to me as the source to meet their emotional need, I feel...

7. I often attempt to control how my emotional need is met by...

CHAPTER TWO

HISTORY

What's Your Story?

I NSIDE EACH OF US LIVES A STORY made up of the relationships and experiences that impact how we function. Connecting with our story has the power to bring great clarity, discovery, and freedom. By contrast, leaving our story buried creates confusion and bondage. Maya Angelou said it best: "There is no greater agony than bearing an untold story inside you."

Your story belongs to you and you alone. It is sacred, deserving of attention and respect. Acknowledging the significance of your journey up to this point is a great step in valuing yourself. Your story matters. It gives you the insight needed to connect the vital dots, creating the pathway for God's healing. Discovering and connecting with your story is not an endeavor of making excuses and shifting blame for your present problems. This would only make your days darker when you are in need of light.

As we tell our stories, we must go deeper than simply stating facts. We need to acknowledge the steady principle of cause and effect. Events and themes from our past have formed the beliefs, emotions, and behaviors we have allowed to govern our souls. We cannot simply stop with asking, "What happened?" Several crucial questions must come next. "What did I believe?" "What did I feel?" "What patterns of behavior were formed by what happened?"

Answering these questions is necessary to exploring our stories in depth. By answering them, we clearly discover how our false selves have been developed, the distorted beliefs that need to be driven out by the truth, emotional healing, and the change in behavior that naturally follows. As you look back into your past, you may be examining some parts of it for the first time. Allow what is hidden in the dark to be brought into the light. Please do not hesitate to seek a counselor or a trusted friend to help you.

As humans, our natural tendency is to avoid pain at all costs. For example, if a child accidentally lays his hand on a hot stove, he will first quickly pull his hand away to get as far from the heat as possible. Then he will clench the hand closely to his chest in an attempt to protect the burn. He will be reluctant to open his hand and reveal the wound, even to receive care from someone who wants to help. This pattern of retreat and protect is typical with physical as well as emotional pain. We protect and hide our wounds, hoping to avoid further pain. Even though we deceive ourselves into thinking we've escaped from the hurt temporarily, time plus stress will wake us up to the reality that our unhealed wounds follow us wherever we go.

If we want change, freedom, and healing, we must do something in complete opposition to our natural instinct. We must run to the pain, fight for the pain, lean into the pain – we must let our wounds be exposed. As children, we retreated from pain in order to survive because we did not have the proper tools to deal with our wounds. While this survival technique may have been a gift from God necessary for a time, as adults, He wants us to live a new way. He never intended for us to live a life of covering up and ignoring our pain. That is why this method no longer works for us. Rest assured, though, if God is leading us to face our pain, He is with us in the process.

We know unclenching our hands and sharing our wounds can be terrifying. All of us have dark places in our history. We have memories we would prefer to forget, wounds that cause deep pain, and regrettable actions that produce guilt and profound sorrow. Now is the time to confront the tension you feel about whether to face your pain

> TIME PLUS STRESS WILL WAKE US UP TO THE REALITY THAT OUR UNHEALED WOUNDS FOLLOW US WHEREVER WE GO.

or leave it buried. This vulnerability is worth it. Those "hard to talk about" memories hold the weight. They reveal the infection. Every step of honesty leads us one step closer to freedom.

The process of healing begins with uncovering the events that shape us. Some of us can easily identify our rejections and wounds. Others of us do not have any events we consider severe or relative to our problems. Nevertheless, we all have been rejected either obviously or subtly and carry the weight of those wounds in our soul.

Imagine two guys, Steve and Oscar. Steve can readily name the wounds from his past affecting him today. At the age of five, he was molested by an uncle; at the age of ten, his parents divorced; and at the age of twenty-two, Steve was fired from the job he loved. These obvious forms of rejection are easily identifiable.

Oscar, on the other hand, can remember no big wounds. However, he does remember many subtle events from the past, including a teacher embarrassing him in front of his friends in second grade; his mom comparing his academic performance to a genius cousin's; being second string in every sport he played; his parents' frequent criticism of the way he dressed; being dumped by his high school girlfriend, who then started dating his friend; and not receiving birthday cards from his grandmother on several occasions, even though she never forgot his brother's birthday. Unlike Steve's obvious rejections, Oscar's subtle rejections are not as easy to identify.

To better understand the significance of wounds, let's equate them to weight with obvious wounds each weighing five pounds and subtle wounds weighing one pound. Steve experienced three obvious wounds, so he is carrying fifteen pounds of wounds in his soul. Oscar experienced fifteen subtle wounds, so he is also carrying fifteen pounds of weight in his soul. Even though Oscar's wounds were more subtle, he experienced enough of them that he is being affected by multiple, smaller wounds just as much as Steve is being affected by fewer but larger wounds and rejections.

What is rejection? It is the absence of meaningful love, love that is significant, purposeful, and substantial. There are many different ways to make someone feel loved, and each of us tends to have a handful of these ways that speak to us as individuals. However, if love is shown to us in a way we are incapable of recognizing, we may perceive this deficit as rejection. For example, if your father's way of showing love was providing for you by working two jobs so he was rarely at home, but you view quality time as love, you might perceive his absence as rejection and not be able to interpret his hard work as love.

Love is the most nourishing, edifying, compelling force, whereas love's adversary, rejection, is the most impoverishing, destructive, repelling force. When the bonds of love are broken, we tend to build walls and isolate our hearts in an attempt to avoid being rejected again. We carry these walls into every relationship we have.

To start you on the path to uncovering your wounds, we have provided a partial list of both obvious and subtle rejections. These can result from any relationship, including but not limited to parents, grandparents, caregivers, siblings, extended family, spouses, girlfriends/boyfriends, friends, classmates, teachers, coaches, spiritual leaders, authority figures, and ourselves.

Some of the wounds or rejections you have experienced may include:

Physical abuse	*Shamed*
Physical intimidation	*High expectations*
Excessive punishment	*Compared to others*
Sexual abuse	*Pressure to perform*
Allowed to see inappropriate material	*Performance-based acceptance*
	Favoritism
Exposed to sexual comments or jokes	*Humiliated*
	Embarrassed
Uncomfortable physical contact	*Bullied*
Verbal abuse	*Picked on*
Mental or emotional abuse	*Made fun of*
Outbursts of anger	*Prejudice*
Criticized	*Gender discrimination*
Put down	*Parents wanted other gender*
Talked down to	*Unresolved arguments in the home*
	Divorce

Death	*Being used*
Critical illness	*Being lied to*
Habitual sickness	*Taken for granted*
Neglect	*Unfaithfulness*
Abandonment	*Not being pursued*
Lack of time spent	*Not being included*
Not being noticed	*Not being chosen*
Lack of affirmation	*Broken promises*
Lack of physical care	*Break up*
Overprotected	*Passed over for promotion, recognition, or award*
Enabled	
Over indulged	*Job loss*
No/little discipline	*Lack of affection*
No/little guidance	*Being ignored*
Excessive lenience	*Silent treatment*
Over-controlling	*Cold shoulder*
Manipulated	*Being slighted*
	Discounting or dismissing emotions

Undoubtedly, as we see particular events on the list that happened to us, we will feel pain. However, it is crucial that we understand the difference between feeling the pain of what actually happened as opposed to feeling pain from lies formed by what happened.

For example, when Jennifer was a young girl, her parents divorced. She spent occasional weekends and holidays with her father, but he was always preoccupied with work and paid very little attention to her. When Jennifer was twelve, her father remarried and had a child with his second wife. He would frequently postpone or cancel plans with Jennifer because of his new obligations.

Even before her father's remarriage, Jennifer believed he had no interest in her. Afterwards, when spending time with her became even less of a priority, her father's attitude left Jennifer feeling neglected, abandoned, and alone. Over time, Jennifer started to believe she was unlovable and unworthy of anyone's time or attention. As Jennifer came of age, she started looking to boys to get her needs met and found herself using sex to gain the attention and acceptance she craved so desperately. She continued this pattern even as an adult, doing whatever was necessary to gain and hold men's attention, neglecting her own needs until she was left feeling like a doormat everyone had wiped their feet on.

Sometimes, Jennifer would attend church, hoping if she did enough of the right things she could alleviate the guilt over her relationship choices and ease the aching longing inside her that never seemed to go away. This seemed to work for a few weeks or months at a time. But she never seemed to make the connections she wanted, nor could she fully absorb the church's messages about God's love because her feelings of worthlessness would always resurface. Then she would begin a new relationship that would give her a more immediate feeling of belonging, and she would wander away from the church, beginning the cycle all over again.

By the time she was thirty, Jennifer had a string of failed relationships behind her. Whenever she took the time to stop and wonder why none of them lasted very long, Jennifer would revert back to what she had believed since childhood: "I am not important. I am not worthy of anyone's time, love, or attention." She believed no matter how hard she tried, no man, no friend, no church, not even God, would ever think she was important, lovable, and worthy enough to care about.

What Jennifer did not realize was she had developed a distorted belief system. Based on her father's treatment of her, Jennifer believed she was not worth anyone's time or attention and that her needs were less important than those of the people around her. Even though Jennifer's father had many faults, it does not benefit her to place the blame for her problems on him. Freedom for Jennifer comes through taking responsibility for her beliefs and her behaviors.

Now Jennifer feels tremendous pain based on not only the lies she has believed about her worthlessness and unlovability but also the rejection at the center of these lies. The goal of identifying all the lies and distorted beliefs is not to keep from feeling pain, but to feel pain for the right thing, grieving a true loss, not the lies that grew out of false beliefs about the loss. For Jennifer, this means peeling away the lies about her worthlessness so she can begin to see herself and her rejections not from her own wounded perspective, but through God's eyes. Peace, love, and freedom come as Jennifer's distorted beliefs begin to be stripped away and the truth is revealed. Once the lie-based pain is removed, Jennifer can then grieve the loss of her relationship with her father and move toward forgiving him.

> SOMETIMES, THE ONLY WAY TO MOVE FORWARD IS TO LOOK BACKWARD.

While we all do not have the same history as Jennifer, we all can relate to rejection, lie-based pain, and the behaviors that follow. As with Jennifer, our distorted beliefs are the factory producing the thoughts and emotions we deal with on a daily basis. We all struggle with negative self-talk pulling us in a dozen different directions. The problem is that thoughts are not where the chaos ends. We find ourselves experiencing all the emotions of self-talk as well. We can exhaust ourselves by trying to control our thoughts and manage our emotions using a variety of self-help tips and tricks. Or we can cooperate with the Holy Spirit and experience the healing that comes when He exposes our distorted beliefs and replaces them with divine truth.

Allowing your story to be drawn out of the shadows into the light can be uncomfortable, to say the least. However, the discomfort is worth the understanding you gain. As the dots begin to connect, you will be able to answer some questions that have been causing you a great deal of confusion, such as, "Why do I feel the way I do?" and "Why do I keep making the same mistakes over and over?" Sometimes, the only way to move forward is to look backward. Being intimately connected with your story is one of the first steps toward walking into the new life you've been craving.

May you become intimately connected with your past, and may you hold it close without letting it hold you back.

Prayer

Father, I own my story and see it as sacred, the way You do. I do not want to minimize my wounds, no matter how large or small, as they are a part of my story. Help me, Father, to face the pain I've been leaning away from. Clearly reveal the lies formed from my past so I can begin to know myself through Your truth. Amen.

JOURNAL QUESTIONS

1. Review the list of wounds and rejections that appears earlier in this chapter. Which ones stand out the most for you? Who are the people associated with those wounds and rejections?

2. Do you find yourself rejecting others in the same ways you were rejected? Or do you find yourself going overboard to avoid rejecting others as you were rejected? Explain.

FURTHER EXERCISES

One of the clearest ways to see how our rejections lead to distorted beliefs, negative feelings, and hurtful behaviors is to create a chart. Here are sample charts for the people used as examples in this chapter, Steve, Oscar, and Jennifer.

STEVE

EVENTS AND THEMES	BELIEF	EMOTION	BEHAVIOR
Molested by uncle	I'm dirty	Shame	Escape through comic books
Parents divorced	I'm not safe	Anxious	Escape through video games
Bullied at school	I'm weak	Embarrassed	Learned to fight
Girlfriend cheated	I'm not enough	Hurt	Found love through rebound relationships
Lost job	I'm not enough	Hurt, angry	Use of alcohol

OSCAR

EVENTS AND THEMES	BELIEF	EMOTION	BEHAVIOR
Teacher embarrassed him in front of friends	I'm a joke	Embarrassed	Self-depreciate
Mom compared him to cousin	I'm not good enough	Shame	Perform for acceptance
Parents were critical	I'm not acceptable	Hurt, angry	Rebel
Girlfriend broke up with him	I'm worthless	Rejected	Take drugs
Grandmother forgot his birthday	I'm forgettable	Hurt	Gave her cold shoulder

JENNIFER

EVENTS AND THEMES	BELIEF	EMOTION	BEHAVIOR
Father ignored her	I'm unlovable	Neglected	Become a people pleaser
Father favored his new family	I'm not important	Abandoned	Act out for attention
Abused by boyfriend	I'm worthless	Hurt, scared	Deny reality of abuse
Unable to maintain relationships	I'm a failure	Shame, loneliness	Avoid connecting with others
Sexually promiscuous	I'm a whore	Shame	Use religious activities to try to cover shame

Following the examples above, create your own charts in your journal. Completing these charts is a sacred endeavor. Ask the Holy Spirit to guide you back to the times in question. Let go of any need to complete the charts perfectly. Tracing your way from significant events and recurring themes in your life, through the beliefs and feelings that developed from those events and themes, to the behaviors that resulted, is not about perfection; it's about revelation. While many events and themes may come to mind immediately as you begin to complete these charts, you should also expect to remember additional events as you continue to process through the rest of this book. When this occurs, return to these charts and add anything else that comes to mind.

1. In the first column of the chart, list the events and themes that have had the greatest effects on your life.

2. In the second column, list the beliefs about yourself, others, life, etc., formed by these events and themes. Some examples of these beliefs may include but are not limited to:

   I am not good enough, I am worthless, I am not important, I am weak, I must be strong, I must be in control, I must be responsible for other people, I must be independent, I am defective.

3. In the third column, list the emotions that accompanied these events and beliefs. If you need help identifying what you were feeling, here are some possibilities:

   Sad (depressed, devastated, embarrassed, hurt, lonely, unloved)

   Angry (bitter, frustrated, resentful)

   Confused (anxious, helpless, hopeless)

Scared (afraid, frightened, insecure)

Weak (ashamed, guilty, inadequate, overwhelmed, powerless, small, stupid, useless, worthless).

4. In the fourth column, list the behaviors that developed from these events, beliefs, and feelings. For example, you may have noticed a tendency to:

Hide	Be passive
Perform for acceptance	Take care of others
Be defensive	Walk on eggshells
Be aggressive	Escape through sex, drugs, alcohol, TV, work, etc.
Procrastinate	

CHAPTER THREE

EXPECTATIONS
System Failure

"MY HAPPINESS GROWS in direct proportion to my acceptance, and in inverse proportion to my expectations," actor Michael J. Fox once stated in an interview with Esquire magazine. The number of people who actually experience a life of freedom apart from expectations is tragically small. We intuitively know that we are forced to deal with a lot of baggage when expectations rule our lives. Instead of having the awareness and courage to explore a life apart from expectations, we try our best to make them work for us. Unfortunately, expectations are an unavoidable part of our society, and a great deal of damage is done when expectations are the standard we use to determine or view who we are.

One might argue areas such as school and work have a place for healthy expectations. However, it is painfully obvious expectations in relationships can only lead to conflict and frustration.

Does this destructive formula sound familiar?

WHAT I DO + MY SUCCESS AT WHAT I DO +
YOUR OPINION OF WHAT I DO = WHO I AM

When we look to our behavior and other people's opinions of our behavior to determine who we are, we must have a way of gauging our successes and failures. Therefore, we measure how well we are doing by submitting to an inexhaustible expectation system. Living in a system of expectations has become so engrained in our culture that we believe the system is normal and even necessary.

For example, Bob felt he had to live up to the expectations of his parents, coaches, and teachers. During the times when he was performing well, he felt lovable and valuable. But whenever Bob failed to live up to the expectations of others, he felt unlovable and worthless. Unknowingly, Bob adopted the common belief system: "If I succeed, I am a success. If I fail, I am a failure." Notice the phrase "I am." In other words, success or failure is not what I do, it's who I am. This lie has contaminated virtually every area of our society.

As we grow up, we become accustomed to connecting failure with shame. We intuitively avoid activities where we anticipate failure, instead searching long and hard for pursuits where we can succeed. This pattern is demonstrated in the movie *Gladiator* when Commodus enters his father's tent after battle, prepared to receive the news that he will be named the next emperor. Instead, his father, Marcus, devastates Commodus by telling him the power will pass to someone else. Commodus says to Marcus, "You wrote to me once, listing the four chief virtues—wisdom, justice, fortitude, and temperance. As I read the list, I knew I had none of them. But I have other virtues, Father—ambition, that can be a virtue when it drives us to excel; resourcefulness; courage, perhaps not on the battlefield, but there are many forms of courage; devotion, to my family, to you. But none of my virtues were on your list."

Knowing he couldn't meet his father's expectations, Commodus created another list through which he knew he could succeed. Filled with anger and suffering from deep depression, Commodus spends the rest of the movie trying to create an identity as Caesar and win the love of Rome. His suffering was the result of a pervasive pattern: The higher the expectation, the higher the anger. The higher the anger, the higher the depression. What peace might Commodus have found if he had entered into a love not based on performance or abilities?

We are all guilty of attempting to gain love and identity as Commodus did. We live much of our lives on the treadmill of performance, chained to a system that will never bring life.

Because living under the expectation system seems so normal, when we begin to ponder the ways of God, we assume He works under the same system. We believe God expects us to perform such activities as reading the Bible, going to church, tithing, witnessing, praying, being helpful, serving, and being good. While all these activities can be a part of our relationship with God, they are not a checklist we must complete in order to have a relationship with Him.

> **THE HIGHER THE EXPECTATION, THE HIGHER THE ANGER. THE HIGHER THE ANGER, THE HIGHER THE DEPRESSION.**

When we succeed at fulfilling our assumed expectations from God, we will feel lovable and valuable, and now, because God is a factor in the equation, we will feel proud and righteous to the level we have met these expectations. Consequently, when we fail, we will feel unrighteous and ashamed to the level of our failure. Any time we perform to try to gain a sense of righteousness, we are guilty of self-righteousness. Self-righteous behavior is far more prevalent than we realize, and it robs us of intimacy with God.

Expectations and intimacy cannot coexist. One will drive away the other. This principle holds true in every relationship, even our relationship with God. If we place expectations on another person, or if we feel they have expectations of us, that system leads to fear of judgment. When we are judging another person, or afraid of being judged ourselves, we cannot maintain healthy relationships, because real relationships cannot thrive in a system that focuses on another person's behavior.

When expectations are used to try to control behavior, we may initially get the results we want. Eventually, though, trying to control with expectations will lead to some form of rebellion and thus produce the opposite of what we intended. The expectation system may seem to be working on the surface; however, it always produces adverse effects, even if these only happen in secret.

LIFE-CHANGE HAPPENS WHEN WE ALLOW THE EXPECTATION SYSTEM TO UTTERLY FAIL.

For example, Alice's husband, Todd, kept a tight control on the family's finances, giving her an allowance for household expenses and expecting her to account for every penny so his money and hard work weren't being wasted. The more tightly Todd tried to control the family's money, and by extension, Alice, the more she resented him. She found herself buying items for the house that weren't strictly necessary, although she told Todd they were; then she would return the items for cash. Alice didn't buy anything with the money. She didn't even know why she wanted it, since she and Todd lived quite comfortably. She just felt the need to have a secret stash, something of her own that her husband didn't know about, to give her a little feeling of control in an area where she otherwise had none.

We all find ways of rebelling against expectations we cannot meet or are tired of attempting to meet. But how can we maintain a close relationship with someone when we are rebelling against the expectations they've placed on us? Or conversely, how can another person maintain a close relationship with us while rebelling against the expectations we've placed on them? True intimacy is about loving and accepting someone for who they are, not what they do or don't do.

Thankfully, God's love for and acceptance of us is in no way based on our performance. He loves us just the way we are, not as the expectation system tells us we should be. If we are performing to gain God's love, acceptance, and approval, then we are wasting effort trying to obtain what we've always had.

Being free from the expectation system does not mean we shut down our passions and goals. We must learn to pay attention to our desires without attaching expectations to them. Our desires are the compass of our souls, leading us down the path of a life filled with purpose. When we live by expectations, our focus is on ourselves and others, and our lives are filled with pressure. Let us adopt the words of the psalmist, David, as our mantra: "Delight yourself in the Lord, and He will give you the desires of your heart" (Psalm 37:4). As we love, delight, and surrender to God, His desires become our desires, and we are safe to boldly ask the question: What do I want?

Imagine the freedom of waking up tomorrow morning and stepping into a life of grace, one in which you are not controlled by expectations you place on yourself or receive from others. A life in which you love and accept others as they are, without placing expectations on them. Can you see yourself resting in the grace of having no expectations of God and knowing He has placed none on you? Life-change happens when we allow the expectation system to utterly fail. Rather than being limited by boundaries, we find ourselves propelled and influenced by love and freedom. As expectations die, our dreams are resurrected.

May you experience the freedom of putting expectations to rest, and may grace awaken the true desires of your heart.

PRAYER

Father, reveal to me the conflict and frustration I have allowed expectations to cause in my relationships. I know the expectation system is normal in my culture, but I don't want to be normal. Please help me to allow this system to utterly fail. I do not want the anger and depression that follow a life of expectations. I want to live a life of freedom, and I want to follow the desires of my heart—and give others permission to do the same. Amen.

In Your Journal...

1. How has this formula affected you?

   **WHAT I DO + MY SUCCESS AT WHAT I DO +
   YOUR OPINION OF WHAT I DO = WHO I AM**

2. Answer each of the following questions.

   Who has placed expectations on you (past and present)? What were those expectations?

   Who have you placed expectations on? What were those expectations?

   What expectations have you placed on God?

   What expectations do you assume God has placed on you?

3. In what ways have expectations robbed you of feeling close with others? With God?

4. Describe what your emotional and mental life would feel like if you woke up tomorrow morning free from expectations from others and on others.

Further Exercises

Think about the people on whom you have placed expectations. Prayerfully consider contacting some or all of these people individually. Apologize for placing these expectations on them and ask for forgiveness.

Identify any expectations you've had of God. In a prayer, let your expectations of Him go and express to Him all your desires.

Chapter Four

The False Self
The Real Problem

RYING TO BLAME OUR PROBLEMS on our current circumstances is an utter waste of time and energy, yet we all do it. We tell ourselves if our circumstances change, our problems will dissolve and we will be happy. We change jobs, find a new spouse or lover, acquire more possessions, move to another town, lose weight, go back to school, change churches, develop new friendships, or experiment with different mind-altering chemicals. Typically, with each change we experience an increase in happiness, a measure of hope for a better life, and a decrease of longing in our souls; however, the relief is always temporary. Eventually, we find ourselves looking for another change, another bit of hope, something or someone to fill the unavoidable gap within each of us and to satisfy the ache in our souls.

Our circumstances are not the problem. Lasting peace cannot be found through making outward changes. No matter how parched our souls may be, nothing from the outside can truly quench our thirst. Everything and everyone we turn to in order to get our needs met eventually fail us. We continue to waste our lives and hurt those we love as well as ourselves until brokenness has its way and we decide to live from a new source.

This problem inside of us has been called many names, including imposter, poseur, impersonator, façade, ego, masquerader, and the flesh. We refer to this problem as the **false self**. Over the course of our lives, all the lies and distorted views we believe about ourselves, God, life, and others, blend together to form our false selves. The false self needs to be exposed and revealed before our true selves can be discovered.

If love is the most healing force we can experience, fear is the most crippling. Fear drives the false self to control. This problem is not a new one; it has been around since the time of Adam and Eve.

Our imaginations can barely grasp the beauty of Adam and Eve's union with God before they decided to take their lives into their own hands. Before fear and shame entered their souls, they were filled with the love and security of their Creator and had no regrets, no remorse, no distorted views of themselves or God. Only authentic relationships and a union of spirits. This is our original design. To live free. To give love and receive love as naturally as breathing, with no insecurities to hinder intimacy. However, freedom is phony and love is illusion unless a choice is offered between surrendering to a safe relationship or resisting love with an attitude of self-reliance.

Adam and Eve chose to resist and take a path of independence from God. In one moment, their eyes were opened to the conflict they had created. They were overcome with fear and shame. As their minds filled with distorted beliefs about themselves and God, their false selves jumped into action. Heartbroken and scared, they hid from God, beginning the task of attempting to deal with their fear and cover their shame through their own strength and resources.

However, Adam and Eve discovered the impossibility of regaining that deep sense of love and union through their attempts at control. No matter how talented we are at sewing fig leaves, they will never remove our fear or cover our shame.

Thankfully, God's love for Adam and Eve and His desire for relationship with them was more powerful than their transgression. He found and restored them by revealing that He and He alone was able to ease their fears and cover their shame.

Adam and Eve set the course for all of humanity to follow. We are born into this world totally self-absorbed yet having no concept of self; therefore, everything is a mirror. We put ourselves at the center of our own experience and begin to interpret the world through the lens of our fear. As with Adam and Eve, our fear motivates us to try to live independently from God and get our need for love met through our own methods of control. All of this snowballs down a hill of conflict and frustration until we finally crash at the bottom and fall apart.

> NO MATTER HOW TALENTED WE ARE AT SEWING FIG LEAVES, THEY WILL NEVER REMOVE OUR FEAR OR COVER OUR SHAME.

Unfortunately, we believe we must be in control in order to be happy, safe, content, loved, and pain free. In the deepest part of our being, we all long for peace and authentic relationships. Unfortunately, we cannot have both control and peace. Choosing one drives out the other.

Allowing our false selves to die so we may find peace through the awakening of our true selves is a transformation that does not happen by simply modifying our behavior. Modifying behavior is attempting to change from the outside in. Real, lasting change happens from the inside out by experiencing revelation and healing. Nevertheless, we need to be able to recognize our actions and choices when living from our false self. Although behavior is not our primary concern, it will reveal to us whether we seek control because of fear or seek peace through surrender.

Even though the origin, motive, and definition of the false self are the same for everyone, our unique behaviors can vary from day to day depending on our circumstances. Below is a list of common behaviors that are a result of living from the false self. Shame, regret, and embarrassment can make it difficult to face our behaviors, but doing so is a crucial step on the pathway to freedom. Take care to identify behaviors you struggle with now as well as those you have struggled with in the past, because we often shift from one behavior to another without ever experiencing healing. Identifying these underlying patterns is important.

Place a C in the box for each behavior that applies to you Currently. Place a P in the box for each behavior that does not currently apply to you but did in the Past. Leave blank any that do not apply and have never applied to you. If you have behaviors not included on this list, write them in the blanks provided at the end.

When you are living from your false self, you may:

- ☐ Keep busy to avoid feelings of inadequacy
- ☐ Work hard to prove your value to others or to God
- ☐ Work hard to compensate for faults or shortcomings

- [ ] Use busyness (work, school, hobbies, other activities) to escape from or avoid dealing with your problems
- [ ] Use busyness to keep people at a distance
- [ ] Use busyness to avoid uncomfortable situations
- [ ] Use busyness as an excuse to stay away from home

- [ ] Be easily influenced by peer pressure
- [ ] Frequently compare yourself to others
- [ ] Change the way you talk to fit the company you are in
- [ ] Change your appearance to be similar to those you want to be accepted by
- [ ] Tell people what they want to hear
- [ ] Compromise your values and integrity to fit in or be accepted
- [ ] Engage in reckless behavior
- [ ] Make decisions that are out of character
- [ ] Put commitments with friends ahead of commitments with God

- [ ] Be described as loud
- [ ] Be described as rude
- [ ] Tend to talk over others
- [ ] Be described as stubborn
- [ ] Be described as argumentative
- [ ] Be described as defensive
- [ ] Be described as unteachable
- [ ] Believe your thoughts and opinions are more important than others'

- ☐ Be described as bossy or pushy
- ☐ Be described as overbearing
- ☐ Make others feel weak and/or wrong so you can control them
- ☐ Be described as critical
- ☐ Be described as demanding
- ☐ Have high expectations of others
- ☐ Be described as intimidating
- ☐ Be described as aggressive
- ☐ Be described as manipulative
- ☐ Arrange circumstances to get your preferred outcome
- ☐ Demand your rights
- ☐ Be afraid to lose control of situations
- ☐ Have difficulty acknowledging and/or respecting authority

- ☐ Be described as harsh
- ☐ Be described as hateful
- ☐ Be described as belligerent
- ☐ Be described as cruel
- ☐ Be described as violent
- ☐ Be described as brutal
- ☐ Tend to overreact
- ☐ Possess a quick temper
- ☐ Keep others anticipating your next outburst of anger
- ☐ Be described as abrasive
- ☐ Be described as cynical

- ☐ Be described as physically overpowering or use your physical presence to intimidate
- ☐ Shut others down
- ☐ Be verbally abusive
- ☐ Be physically abusive
- ☐ Bully others
- ☐ Ignore the long term consequences of your actions
- ☐ View and treat ordinary circumstances as threatening, disrespectful, and/or offensive

- ☐ Anticipate the needs of others
- ☐ Make decisions for others
- ☐ Take responsibility for the lives of others
- ☐ Become too involved in the lives of others
- ☐ Take responsibility for other people's actions
- ☐ Take responsibility for other people's feelings
- ☐ Be easily influenced by others' needs
- ☐ Give unsolicited advice
- ☐ Rescue others from failure
- ☐ Be overprotective
- ☐ Do things for others they should do for themselves
- ☐ Try to be all things to all people
- ☐ Try to make everyone happy
- ☐ Nag or lecture others
- ☐ Enable others
- ☐ Keep secrets for others

☐ Rescue others from facing the consequences of their actions

☐ Make excuses for others

☐ Not place blame in the appropriate place

☐ Lack objectivity

☐ Have a warped sense of responsibility

☐ Worry frequently about the possibility of someone being upset with you

☐ Worry about what others think

☐ Become anxious or guilty when other people have a problem

☐ Become angry when your help isn't effective

☐ Say "yes" when you should say "no"

☐ Do things you really don't want to be doing

☐ Feel and act like a door mat

☐ Complain about feeling underappreciated

☐ Avoid engaging people

☐ Attempt to be unseen and unheard

☐ Procrastinate

☐ Give up or quit easily

☐ Appear lazy and lethargic

☐ Wait for others to do things for you

☐ Avoid necessary confrontation

☐ Avoid making decisions

☐ Avoid difficult situations

☐ Avoid expressing needs

- [ ] Frequently make remarks like "it doesn't matter to me" and "whatever you want is fine with me"
- [ ] Avoid risk
- [ ] Look to others to tell you what to do and how to think
- [ ] Hide your true feelings and thoughts
- [ ] Rarely express your own opinion
- [ ] Avoid failure at all cost
- [ ] Struggle to engage and be present with others
- [ ] Give others the silent treatment
- [ ] Strive to keep peace when tension is needed
- [ ] Apologize when you have done nothing wrong
- [ ] Shift all responsibility to others

- [ ] Downplay personal successes, gifts, and talents
- [ ] Avoid or procrastinate on projects that might lead to success or recognition
- [ ] Not follow dreams in order to avoid anxiety
- [ ] Self-sabotage (perhaps in subtle ways) when things are going well
- [ ] Believe you are unworthy of success
- [ ] Avoid getting your hopes up for fear of being disappointed
- [ ] Avoid success, fearing that success is not sustainable even when achieved
- [ ] Make excuses for not pursuing opportunities

☐ Function under religious law and use it to measure goodness or badness by comparing performance to the demands of the law

☐ Be judgmental, especially of those who do not meet religious expectations

☐ Use religious guilt to control others

☐ Act as God's police

☐ Perform religious activities in hopes of gaining approval from God and/or people

☐ Attempt to gain a sense of righteousness (right standing with God) through religious activities

☐ Frequently mention religious activities and accomplishments

☐ Serve God out of obligation rather than love

☐ Manipulate others through quoting Scripture

☐ Blame Satan for any difficulty

☐ Use religious phrases to appear more spiritual

☐ Place demands on God

☐ Use religious activity as an escape

☐ Make sexual propositions

☐ Play off sexual behavior as innocent when confronted

☐ Make inappropriate comments

☐ Give inappropriate compliments

☐ Frequently solicit compliments

☐ Overshare sexual issues

☐ Give lingering hugs, stares, and/or touches

- ☐ Dress in a manner that is provocative or designed to display the body
- ☐ Overuse makeup, perfume, or cologne
- ☐ Manipulate others by offering sex or using sex as a reward
- ☐ Use sexual activity to escape from problems or stress
- ☐ Escape through pornography and/or fantasy
- ☐ Escape through masturbation

- ☐ Focus on your suffering and trials to get attention from others
- ☐ Self-depreciate in order to get attention
- ☐ Minimize your abilities
- ☐ Act as if you are owed something by others
- ☐ Engage in self-pity
- ☐ Play the role of the victim and/or martyr
- ☐ Take things too personally
- ☐ Set yourself up to be rejected
- ☐ Inaccurately perceive rejection
- ☐ Focus on potential catastrophe instead of reality
- ☐ Become obsessed with the past
- ☐ Worry excessively about the future

- ☐ Avoid social situations
- ☐ Distance yourself from others
- ☐ Avoid relationships

- [ ] Avoid intimacy
- [ ] Escape through avoidance
- [ ] Be unapproachable
- [ ] Retreat into a shell
- [ ] Become a loner
- [ ] Avoid certain people
- [ ] Not communicate
- [ ] Be aloof or unapproachable
- [ ] Be indifferent or lack empathy
- [ ] Appear uncaring or act unconcerned
- [ ] Escape through sleeping

- [ ] Use alcohol to escape from problems or stress
- [ ] Use illegal drugs as an escape
- [ ] Overuse or misuse prescription drugs
- [ ] Escape through fantasy or daydreaming
- [ ] Escape through cutting or self-harm
- [ ] Escape by becoming overly focused on food, eating, or dieting
- [ ] Use exercise to avoid problems
- [ ] Become overly focused on appearance
- [ ] Escape through entertainment (TV, movies, video games, internet, social media, reading)
- [ ] Use shopping as an escape
- [ ] Focus on material possessions and/or status
- [ ] Escape through talking or socializing

☐ _____

☐ _____

☐ _____

☐ _____

☐ _____

In Chapter 2, you may have encountered some difficulties identifying the behaviors formed by your significant events and themes of rejection. Now that you have completed this checklist, it may be helpful for you to review the charts you filled out for Chapter 2 and connect more of your behaviors with the events and themes that led to them.

Using this list to take a hard look at our behavior can be overwhelming. While it is important to embrace the conviction that comes from our harmful behavior being exposed, it is equally important to remember that our behaviors are symptoms of the problem, not the root of the problem. These behaviors are the fruits of our wounds and our distorted belief systems.

> OVER TIME, OUR FORTS BECOME PRISONS, AND WE CAN'T SEEM TO ESCAPE.

Self-protection and isolation are common impulses behind our false self. As children, we instinctively built forts. We would use anything we could—wood for a fort outside or blankets and boxes for a fort inside. When we could find nothing to use, we would simply retreat to a corner of the closet or under our bed. We built these forts because they kept people out so we could feel safe. So many of the behaviors you identify with on the previous list were at one time forts to help you feel safe, loved, and in control.

The problem is that over time, our forts become prisons, and we can't seem to escape. As our belief systems heal and grow, our strongholds are broken down, and we are able to walk out of the prisons that once held us.

The false self is at the root of our relational difficulties because it is founded on fear, selfishness, self-centeredness, and self-absorption. Take that foundation, mix it with the need to control, and you have a recipe for conflict and frustration, making it impossible to give love selflessly or receive love effortlessly. When living from our false self, we have difficulties seeing and feeling love from other people because they are attempting to love our false self. However, as we discover who we really are, we have the opportunity to make our true selves available for others to love.

IF I AM NOT MY FALSE SELF, THEN WHO AM I?

Because of our insecurities, the false self is constantly trying to draw the life out of others and build an identity instead of abiding in the constant life-flow from God and resting in the true identity He has already given. Like a person agonizing from thirst, we crawl from one mirage to the next seeking relief. We set our expectations and shift our focus from one person to the next, one thing to the next, trying to find that life-giving source who can meet our expectations, make us feel loved, and tell us who we truly are.

All this leads us to various forms of judgment and control, creating a false system through which we attempt to function. We will struggle to make this system work until the pain of staying the same exceeds the pain it will take to change. Letting go of our false selves as well as the sources that have failed us will not happen overnight. Be patient and gentle with yourself as your grip is loosened.

When we choose to build our relationship with God through our false self, we struggle in our effort to develop intimacy with Him. We try to fill the void in our lives with people, things, and status instead of relationship with God. These counterfeit measures become idols, and we devote the best of ourselves to them. We live as though God is merely an afterthought to our daily lives instead of a loving, caring Father who is invested in our hearts. For some, life becomes an effort of trying to control God with our prayers and good works. We see Him as a cosmic vending machine existing solely to give us what we want, when we want it, and how we want it. When this fails us, we become angry, bitter, or indifferent towards Him.

Graciously, we are never an afterthought to God. He is always present and extremely attentive. Regardless of whether we are in the midst of our futile attempts to control or are becoming aware of the truth that our void can only be filled through Him, He loves us unconditionally and thoroughly.

Why is letting go of the false self so difficult? Because even though it creates conflict and frustration, it has become something of a friend. The false self has helped us survive and seemingly gotten us through our pain up to this point, and detachment is never easy. After all, there do seem to be some so-called benefits from living a false life. We had to be getting something out of it, or we never would have lived that way in the first place. Once we realize we are not who we thought we were, a terrifying question often follows: "If I am not my false self, then who am I?" As a result, allowing our awareness of our true selves to be stirred and being awakened to a new life may feel frightening or even counterintuitive for a while. However, the journey is an adventurous one, full of trials and errors, successes and failures as we learn to see with new eyes and experience with new hearts.

May you allow your false self to be drawn out from the shadows, and may you receive the truth that your false self is not the real you.

PRAYER

Father, please remove my tendency to blame my problems on my outward circumstances. Let me taste the freedom that comes when I take full responsibility for myself. I acknowledge my false self may have been necessary for survival as a child, but now my true self longs to experience a life functioning from who I truly am and not the false self I created. Amen.

IN YOUR JOURNAL...

1. Referring to all the behaviors that apply to you from the checklist in this chapter, describe your false self as vividly as possible.

   EXAMPLE 1: "My false self is **passive**, prone to **escape** from stress and pressure through **busyness**. My false self also will **keep people at a distance** by being cynical. My false self is at times abrasive and **controls** people by **being cruel** and forcing others to walk on eggshells around me. In certain situations, my false self **becomes a doormat** and has a **difficult time saying no.** My false self is **self-depreciating** and often **downplays success, gifts, and talents.** My false **self plays the role of victim and martyr** and engages in **self-pity.**"

EXAMPLE 2: "My false self **performs for the acceptance** of God and others. My false self is **prone to compare** itself with others and can be very **defensive when challenged.** My false self becomes **too involved in the lives of others** and tends to **take responsibility for the lives of others.** My false self **enables others** by **making excuses for them** and **keeping their secrets.** My false self attempts to **find its value through accomplishing and achieving goals** instead of in God.

2. How has your false self affected your relationships with others? How has it affected your relationship with God?

3. Are you convinced nothing good can come from your false self? Explain why or why not.

Further Exercise

Write a letter to your false self in which you embrace it for helping you to survive this far, while acknowledging the conflict and frustration you have allowed it to cause. Separate your true self from your false self by telling the latter goodbye. Read your letter out loud to yourself and God. You may also find it helpful to have a trusted friend present as you read the letter.

CHAPTER FIVE

Brokenness

It's a Beautiful Place to Live

T HE SUBJECT OF BROKENNESS is often talked about in religious and spiritual circles. This conversation has been around a long time, and unfortunately for some of us, overexposure to the subject has created a narrow view. We have reduced brokenness to the belief that God is either causing or allowing bad things to happen in order to subtly force us to obey Him. While obedience is a positive thing, reducing brokenness down to obedience is like reducing all of God's creation down to a single flower. Another consequence of this narrow viewpoint on brokenness is that when people hear the term, they associate it with tragic events and the emotional states that follow such as depression and despair. While events, circumstances, and emotions can be components to brokenness, they are simply that, components.

Brokenness is not merely a single event or an emotional state. It is an attitude of dependence we are to *continually live in*. It is acknowledging that we ourselves don't have the resources to live a life of love and peace; rather, we are utterly dependent on God for absolutely everything we need. The attitude of brokenness declares all our methods of control, idols, and false selves to be void of any meaningful purpose in our lives.

Brokenness is hindered when we allow our fear and pride to cause us to try to control when, where, and how our needs are met. Letting go of our false gods and our false selves is difficult. Sometimes we resist brokenness because we are afraid of the love and vulnerability we will feel after all of our walls are dismantled. We become comfortable relying on our own will, and it frightens us to echo the prayer of Jesus: Not my will, but Your will be done. We can become so accustomed to our prisons or mediocre lives that we resist brokenness, afraid of what's on the other side.

We have become experts at preventing ourselves from experiencing brokenness. We use busyness, chemicals, other people. We can even use "good" things such as performing religious activities, volunteering, and helping others. We do all of these things trying to find hope in the midst of our situation, but this is false hope. When it comes to brokenness, hopelessness is not something to avoid; rather, we need to give ourselves over to it. We need to let our false selves break. We need to experience the hopelessness of living from our self-created resources.

> IT FRIGHTENS US TO ECHO THE PRAYER OF JESUS: NOT MY WILL, BUT YOUR WILL BE DONE.

So much of the self-help industry is focused on helping us "find ourselves," but if we follow the steps in most of these books, we are not *finding* ourselves so much as attempting to *make* ourselves. We are taking something else from the outside and using it to polish our layers of false self instead of having them stripped away.

You may find it helpful to think of brokenness in this way: Our false selves are outer shells that must be broken in order for our true selves, infused with God's spirit, to come out into the world. The acorn shell must crack for the tree within to grow. An alabaster box must break to release the aroma of the perfume within. The cocoon must split open in order for the butterfly to emerge. What is outward may have seemed to serve you for a while. However, inside, we are carrying a treasure, and the more we are broken outwardly, the more the treasure is shared with the world. Brokenness is about cracking open all those layers of false self to find out what's always been buried inside. This is what it really means to find yourself.

Our selfishness, self-centeredness, self-motivation, and self-reliance are robbing us and others of what it means to experience an authentic spiritual life. We have kept our true selves locked away behind walls of fear, shame, and the false self. As these walls come down through brokenness, the sweet aroma of who God is comes out, bringing with it everything we truly are as well. Here we find the words of Paul to be so true: There is a treasure inside these jars of clay (II Corinthians 4:7).

Discovering this treasure and living from His riches changes everything. When we choose an attitude of brokenness, we begin to see ourselves and the world around us with our spiritual eyes of love without the lens of fear. We are less interested the temporary and tangible circumstances around us, and we begin to sense what God is doing in the spiritual and intangible realm. This shift in focus brings peace because when we are broken, everything slows down. Fear no longer drives our minds to control and attempt to figure everything out because we are dependent on God to take the lead in every circumstance.

Brokenness is mandatory for real and lasting change. If we are satisfied with our lives exactly the way they are, then we simply need to keep our level of dependence on God where it is. But if we want more of what is true, more of what is real, if we want to live a life of love, peace, and genuine adventure, then WE MUST BE BROKEN. There is a beauty to brokenness, a sweetness. We are broken when we experience a sacredness that cannot be experienced any other way. When we live in a state of dependence and in the freedom

> BROKENNESS IS NOT AN EMOTION FOR US TO TRY TO FIX; IT IS A NAME TO EMBRACE.

that comes from releasing control, we begin to know what it means to walk in the spirit (Galatians 5:16). Over time and with experience, our walk in the spirit becomes a dance. Brokenness has its own rhythm as it becomes a way of life. We experience this dance when we remain in an attitude of dependence, no matter the circumstances. We are to be broken people, on the mountaintops and in the valleys, in our successes and failures, in good times and bad. Brokenness is not an emotion for us to try to fix; it is a name to embrace.

May you allow the beauty of brokenness to have its way with you, and may you experience the joy of living from the inside out.

PRAYER

———

Father, widen my narrow view and allow me to see the complete picture of brokenness. Convince me that all my methods of control are an illusion leading me farther away from where I truly want to be. I embrace the hopelessness that comes from my impulse to control. Take my hand and lead me in the dance of brokenness as I embrace this dance as a lifestyle. I rest in the beauty of being broken with You. Amen.

IN YOUR JOURNAL...

———

1. How have your preconceived notions about brokenness been challenged by this chapter?

2. In what ways do you tend to prevent yourself from experiencing brokenness?

3. What is preventing you from embracing brokenness right now?

4. How would your life be different if you allowed your false self to be broken?

FURTHER EXERCISES

In your journal, draw a picture of a butterfly cocoon. Make it large enough that you can write inside. Now within the cocoon, list the characteristics of your false self that are most in need of being broken.

On the next page of your journal, draw a picture of a butterfly. On the wings of the butterfly, list everything you hope to experience through brokenness (for example, peace, joy, contentment).

CHAPTER SIX

CONCEPT OF GOD
PART I
He's Not Who You Thought He Was

WE CAN ALWAYS DISCOVER what we hold to be important by taking stock of what we invest in and pay the most attention to. Naturally, when it comes to ourselves, we tend to focus on what we can see, such as our appearance. This is unfortunate because the most important elements of our being cannot be seen in a mirror yet still deserve our attention.

Whether we are aware of it or not, our Concept of God, how we view His character, is the most influential part of our psyche. A. W. Tozer said it best: "What comes into our minds when we think about God is the most important thing about us." Our Concept of God affects everything: our thoughts, emotions, behaviors, relationships, worldview. How we view God's character creates the inner environment that impacts how we treat ourselves and others. We continually project our image of God, which lives inside us, outward to the world. Consequently, having a healthy, proper view of God's character is of the utmost importance.

Before we enter into the sacred endeavor of unpacking our Concept of God, we must acknowledge four common hindrances. The first and perhaps easiest hindrance to understand is that many of us have never realized before now our Concept of God even exists. Again, ignoring the intangible parts of us is easy.

A second, more complicated hindrance to having a healthy and fully formed Concept of God arises when we believe focusing on our intellectual thoughts and ideas concerning Him is enough. We need to acknowledge we also have an emotional Concept of God. We know what ideas of Him lay in our minds, but our emotions can often tell us something completely different. For example, we may know intellectually that God is everywhere and we are never outside of His presence. However, we may have seasons when we feel lonely. Over time, we can allow the emotion of loneliness to create a belief we may never admit and confess with our mouth: "God has abandoned me." Unfortunately, we often allow the voice of our emotions to trump what we know to be true. Both our intellectual and emotional Concept of God make up our experience, so we must receive emotional healing along with gaining the proper knowledge of Him.

A third hindrance to understanding our Concept of God can be our fear of honesty. Finding the courage to be truthful about our distorted views of God can be difficult. We may hesitate to make "negative" statements about Him because it seems disrespectful and irreverent. However, being honest is absolutely necessary for growth. God knows our distorted views of Him, and it pleases Him when we feel safe enough to admit them. His shoulders are big enough to handle our questions, doubts, and criticisms.

David, a man whose journey took him from a lowly shepherd to King of Israel, is a good example of someone willing to be honest about his doubts and frustrations with God. The Psalms for the most part are David's journal entries. In Psalm 13:1-4, David honestly questions God: "How long, O Lord? Will you forget me forever? How long will you hide your face from me? How long must I take counsel in my soul and have sorrow in my heart all the day? How long shall my enemy be exalted over me?" David feels alone and begins to wonder if God has turned His back or even forgotten him. Instead of hiding those feelings, David expresses them.

Jesus provides another example of someone close to God who also feels safe enough to be honest with Him. In the Garden of Gethsemane, Jesus begins to prepare Himself to face the torment ahead. Even though He is fully aware what is about to happen will change the world forever, Jesus has a moment of intense emotion leading Him to ask God, "Father, if you are willing, remove this cup from me." Jesus **must** make this request in order to fully accept what must be done. This process of honesty leads Him to make a statement of faith that echoes through all eternity: "Nevertheless, not my will, but yours, be done" (Luke 22:42). Our process of living a life of faith will require us to be honest as well.

> HOW WE VIEW GOD'S CHARACTER CREATES THE INNER ENVIRONMENT THAT IMPACTS HOW WE TREAT OURSELVES AND OTHERS.

We need to feel safe enough to do the same as David and Jesus did. Not only can God handle the expression of doubts about His character, He invites them because He knows honesty leads to intimacy.

All of us are born with absolutely no idea of who God is or what His character is like. Our intellectual and emotional concepts of Him are blank canvases awaiting a masterpiece. Regrettably, the paints we use to create the masterpiece come from a fallen and broken world. While some paints flow onto the canvas and reveal a beautiful image of who God truly is, others taint and distort our concept of Him and what we believe His character to be.

We must be careful to hand the paintbrush to the correct artist: One who adores us and longs to reveal Himself to us. His job is to erase the distorted views and paint new, accurate ones. Our job is to cooperate with Him in the process.

When we commit ourselves to the journey of cooperating with God, we naturally place most of our attention on our intellectual concept of Him. While head knowledge about God is important, we must not ignore the parts of our souls needing a deep connection that knowledge alone cannot

> NOT ONLY CAN GOD HANDLE THE EXPRESSION OF DOUBTS ABOUT HIS CHARACTER, HE INVITES THEM BECAUSE HE KNOWS HONESTY LEADS TO INTIMACY.

provide. We must be careful not to limit our relationship with God to having our facts correct about Him. Focusing on our knowledge of God is too easy. What we really need is a relational connection with Him that transcends information.

When it comes to healing and growing our Concept of God, pride is a fourth major hindrance. We tend to protect our belief systems because we find safety in them. For some of us, our image of God is so firmly planted in our minds that admitting we could be wrong is a bitter pill to swallow. When this happens, we allow only black and white paints to be used, fearing any color that hints towards new names and new revelations. It can be difficult to open our minds up to the possibility of being wrong. However, when we allow grace to absorb our pride and humility to drive out arrogance, we become more teachable. At this point, God can begin to replace our black and white image of Him with a prism of colors.

If we think we have no issues with our Concept of God, we are running the risk of putting the brakes on our spiritual growth. Believing our knowledge about God is complete, with no distorted views that need to be replaced by truth, leads to a stagnant relationship. Growth is a constant process of unlearning and learning, and a real relationship is about continual discovery.

Can we take the risk of beginning or reentering this journey? Can we admit some things we think and feel about the character of God might be distorted and untrue? Can we admit we have a need information alone cannot meet? Addressing these questions can feel like we are risking the perceived security of having God fit in our nice, neat little boxes. Allowing those boxes to be opened, or even realizing the boxes never really existed, can be a challenge for some. The risk is worth it. Admitting our image of God is wrong and incomplete is a step of vulnerability necessary for entering into a deeper knowing.

The healing and growing of our Concept of God is important not only to our peace and freedom, but also to everyone we are in relationship with. For some mysterious reason, God puts much of His reputation in the hands of a fallen world and its broken people. Think about it: we are born with no idea of who God is or what His character is like. People, systems, and our experiences all influence how we think and feel about God.

We find an example of this in the history of the Children of Israel. They suffered severe oppression in Egypt under Pharaoh's rule. God heard their cries for deliverance and sent Moses to rescue them. During the mass exodus from Egypt, the Israelites experienced many mind-blowing miracles as God proved Himself to be faithful to them time and time again. Their journey through the desert was long, but they finally made it to the edge of the Promised Land. Before entering the land God had promised them, they decided to send in spies to investigate. The spies returned and reported the Ammorites who already inhabited the land were big and powerful.

Even though God had proven Himself to be loving and protective, when the Children of Israel faced further adversity, they said, "The Lord hates us; so He brought us out of Egypt to deliver us into the hands of the Ammorites to destroy us" (Deuteronomy 1:27). Since Pharaoh had overbearing expectations of the Children of Israel, they may have assumed God's character was the same as Pharaoh's, a ruthless taskmaster who demanded more of them than they felt they could give. What are some names the Israelites might have had for God? Perhaps they named Him deserting, cruel, malicious, ruthless, overbearing, and unloving.

Just like the Children of Israel's, our Concept of God is formed from our past authority figures and experiences, which is why in certain circumstances we may see God as distant, uncaring, or even punishing. Typically, the people and systems influencing our Concept of God are parents, grandparents, teachers, coaches, friends, church, society, and culture. Even if some of these key people never took us to church or spoke to us about God or the Bible, the simple fact that they were authority figures influenced our Concept of God because we commonly see God through the lens of all previous authority, religious or not.

Here is a list of examples to demonstrate how our Concept of God is shaped by previous authority. While this list is not exhaustive, our goal is to give you enough examples to help you begin discovering how your Concept of God was developed.

PARENTS, GRANDPARENTS, & PRIMARY CAREGIVERS	NAMES OF OR BELIEFS ABOUT GOD
Physically or emotionally absent	God is elsewhere.
Focused on work or busy with other things	God is distracted.
Critical, fault finding attitude	God is judgmental.
Overprotective and lacked confidence in my abilities	God does not believe I am capable.
Unengaged and detached when I was in need	God is passive.
Delivered consequences out of anger	God is punishing.
Treated people unequally	God plays favorites.

TEACHERS & COACHES	NAMES OF OR BELIEFS ABOUT GOD
Emphasized performance over relationship	God is performance based.
Used embarrassment as a tool for correction and/or motivation	God is cruel.
Focused more on results than on me	God is a user.
Taught failure is unacceptable	God is repelled by failure.

CHURCH & RELIGION	NAMES OF OR BELIEFS ABOUT GOD
Leadership seemed frustrated, demanding, and/or impatient.	God is angry.
Rules emphasized more than relationships	God is a taskmaster.
Used fear and shame to correct and motivate	God is controlling.
Insinuated that God has two primary dwelling places: Heaven and church.	God is distant.
Church attendance stressed more than discipleship and daily living.	God is behavior focused.
Preached sermons focused on the torment of hell and how to avoid spending eternity there.	God is punitive.
Taught that God can be controlled through prayer.	God is a vending machine.

SOCIETY & CULTURE	NAMES OF OR BELIEFS ABOUT GOD
Things should come quickly and easily and I should rarely have to wait on anything.	God is holding out on me.
I have the right to be happy and my happiness should be my primary focus.	God is a sugar daddy.
In order to feel loved, accepted, valued, and secure, my physical appearance must meet the standards of society and culture.	God is focused on outward appearance.
Success is defined by the size of my house, the label on my clothes, the maker of my car, and the things I possess.	God is materialistic.

CONCEPT OF GOD PART I

As this list indicates, we develop our Concept of God based in part on our previous experiences with authority. Then we unintentionally project our views about God onto others through our actions and attitudes, so these inaccurate views of God end up affecting our relationships. For example, if a parent feels God is blunt and harsh, they will have a tendency to treat their children the same way they believe God treats them. On the other side of the scale, if a parent believes God is passive and permissive, they will likely parent from a similar attitude, and their children will have a hard time accepting consequences for negative actions.

Sometimes our distorted views of God are formed by traumatic events not directly tied to a specific person or rejection, such as a car accident, sudden illness, or disability. For example, Tony grew up with just a vague sense of who God is. The only thing he ever really heard about God was that He is always in control. You can imagine what happened to Tony's view of God when he lost an arm in a car accident. Instead of turning to God in a personal way, sharing all his real emotions in the aftermath of the tragedy and allowing God to comfort him, Tony simply turned cold and stood behind the statement, "This was God's will for my life." Tony saw himself as a puppet and God as the puppet master. Tony's breakthrough finally came when he discovered God was compassionately connected with him even through the pain and confusion. Once the wall of bitterness came down, Tony was able to process all the difficult questions and

AS OUR CONCEPT OF GOD BEGINS TO HEAL AND GROW, WE WILL SEE OTHERS AND OURSELVES WITH NEW EYES.

doubts about God that arise when a tragedy occurs. Discovering the truth about God's character not only deepened Tony's relationship with Him, it also spared him from a future potentially hindered by his previously distorted view.

Distorted views of God can play out in our lives in many different ways. Covering them all is impossible, but here are some of the most common symptoms we may experience.

SOME SYMPTOMS OF A DISTORTED VIEW OF GOD

Persistent fear	Bitterness
Open rebellion	Not sensing God's love
Often feeling alone	Pattern of living in defeat
Expecting God to be a vending machine	Judgmental attitude toward self, God, and/or others
Resisting brokenness	Often feeling overwhelmed
Often angry	Passive
Controlling	Legalistic
Not taking risks	Lingering confusion
Victim attitude	Often distrusting
Uncaring or callous	Withholding and stingy

As our Concept of God begins to heal and grow, we will see others and ourselves with new eyes. We will notice ourselves beginning to have compassion for those who previously frustrated us. We will find ourselves open to new relationships and willing to restore broken ones. Passion for life will begin to grow as we draw love from God's endless well. To say our lives will transform is not an overstatement.

May you allow the Holy Spirit to open your eyes to how you truly see God, and may the lies you believe about His character be exposed so you can boldly proclaim, "That is not who my God is."

PRAYER

Father, the way I see You and Your character shapes my soul like nothing else does. Allow me to clearly see how my image of You has been developed. Expose all of my distortions concerning Your character. Reveal all that needs to be unlearned. Shine a light on every idea I have about You that does not truly represent You. Break my pride, which makes it difficult to admit I'm wrong, and calm my fear of letting go of who I thought You were. Amen.

In Your Journal...

1. Is it difficult to be honest about your distorted views of God's character? Explain why or why not.

2. Who are the primary people and what are the primary experiences that have influenced your Concept of God in a negative way? What distorted views of God's character did you form from them?

3. Describe two or three of your distorted views about God's character you discovered from reading this chapter.

4. How have your distorted views of God affected your life in a negative way?

Further Exercise

Imagine you have spent years wanting a closer relationship with a certain person, but there always seemed to be an invisible wall between you. Then one day, you discover the reason you were not closer is that you had believed untrue things about this person's character.

One of the first things you would want to do is have a conversation with them, confessing that you had believed lies, apologizing, and describing the relationship you want with them now the misconceptions have been revealed. Even though you never made a conscious choice to believe the lies, some part of our hearts usually feels the need to say, "I'm sorry for believing things that were untrue."

This is a great step to take in your relationship with God. Write a letter to God in which you confess the lies you've believed about Him and apologize. Then tell Him your hopes for the future concerning your relationship with Him.

*C*HAPTER *S*EVEN

CONCEPT OF GOD
PART II
Jesus Pulls Back the Curtain

*T*AKING A HARD LOOK AT HOW WE THINK and feel about
God is clearly the most important and sacred endeavor of our
lives. Once our distorted views of God have been exposed, they must
be replaced with the truth. How do we know what the truth is? Is it
arrogant to say God is knowable? Can we really know God's character?

The answer to the last question is "yes." We can know Him. While
we may never scratch the surface of knowing everything about Him
intellectually, we can know Him in a way that is deeper than our intellect. We can know and touch Him with our love. Where our brains
come up short, our love is able to experience God in a way that allows
us to say with confidence, "I know my Father, and He knows me."
Jesus told Thomas and Philip, "If you really know me, you will know
my father as well. From now on, you do know him and have seen him"
(John 14:7). The writer of Hebrews even declares Jesus to be the radiance of God's glory and the exact representation of His being (1:1-3).

Jesus came to reveal God's character in a way previously hidden from humanity. In the Old Testament, God was referred to as Lord God Almighty, The Most High God, Everlasting God, Lord, Master, etc. He is all of those. He always has been and always will be. However, Jesus came to show us something more. This is best described with the endearing name Jesus called God—Abba, an Aramaic word used in Jesus' day the same way we currently use the words Daddy or Papa. He brought our God from distant to close, from unreachable to approachable, from a voice silent for four hundred years to a constant who longs for conversation and relationship with us.

I KNOW MY FATHER, AND HE KNOWS ME.

Jesus' relationship with His Father is so intimate that when we see Him, we see the exact representation of His Father. Jesus so resembles the Father that He can say they are one. He radiates His Father's glory, and His Father's character flows naturally from Him. This relationship is demonstrated in Hebrews 1:1-3a when the writer says, "In the past God spoke to our ancestors through prophets at many times and in various ways, but in these last days he has spoken to us by his son, whom he appointed heir of all things, and through whom also he made the universe. The son is the radiance of God's glory and the exact representation of his being, sustaining all things by His powerful word."

Jesus Himself told a number of parables to illustrate His Father's character. For example, one day He overheard a group of prominent, well-educated religious leaders murmuring about Him (Luke 15). These men were critical of Jesus because He had been engaging with society's outcasts through the intimate act of sharing a meal. Jesus interrupted

His critics' back biting by telling several stories to reveal His own character as well as His Father's.

The most famous of these stories tells of a father with two sons. The parable begins with the younger son coming to his father in a blatant act of disrespect and disloyalty, demanding the father hand over his portion of the inheritance immediately rather than at his father's death. Basically, the son is saying, "I wish you were dead." The father does not resist. He doesn't shame his son. He doesn't discourage him. With his actions, the father communicates to the son that he is free—free to stay within the safety and comfort of his father's home or free to experience living life his way.

The son leaves home for a distant country. After he wastes all of his money, a severe famine hits the land. Broke and starving, unable to meet his most basic needs through his own resources, he takes a job feeding pigs. In time, the son grows so hungry he even considers eating the pigs' slop. His heart begins to long for what he has lost, and he wants to go back home to his father. He prepares a speech—"Father, I have sinned against heaven and against you. I am no longer worthy to be called your son; make me like one of your hired servants"—and begins to travel home (Luke 15:17b-19).

The father, looking for his son and hoping for his return, sees him coming home from a long way off. Filled with joy, excitement, and relief, the father runs to meet his son, embracing him and welcoming him with a kiss. The son begins his speech; excitedly, the father cuts him off and instructs the servants to bring his best robe, a ring for the son's finger, sandals for the son's feet, and to begin preparations for a celebration. The son returns home thinking himself worthy only to be a hired hand. However, upon his return the father does not give him the tools of a hired hand but rather the significant items that could only confirm him as one thing: his heir. His son.

Just any clothing to cover the son is not enough. The father instructs the servants to bring the best robe to communicate the son's return from poverty to riches, from self-sufficiency to dependence, from being exposed to being covered. Bare feet are markers of poverty and slavery—only slaves and servants went shoeless. Although the son is willing to be a servant, the father immediately places shoes on his son's feet because sin has not diminished the son's value in his father's heart. In those times, the family ring was the equivalent of the family credit card. The ring, bearing the family's crest, was used in the marketplace to purchase goods and services on credit. This son has blown a significant portion of the family fortune. Remarkably, within minutes of his return, the father restores all of his financial privileges and throws a party in his honor. The father does not hide his son in shame. He throws a party. No lectures, no punishment—a celebration.

However, the younger son is not the only one who needs his father. There is an older son equally in need of love. When the younger son returns home, his older brother is in the field working. As the older brother approaches the house, he hears the sounds of a party. He becomes indignant upon discovering his younger brother has returned home and their father is celebrating in his honor. The older brother feels his younger brother has gone on a frivolous adventure and wasted the family's money while he was at home working hard and following the rules. The celebration threatens his belief system of earning. Trapped by the illusion of expectations, he has spent years trying to earn what he did not understand was already his by birth.

The father, deeply sensitive to each son's needs, runs out to greet his rebellious younger son on the road back home from the hog pen and leaves the party to meet his judgmental elder son on the path back home from the fields. The father's hugs and kisses speak grace and acceptance to the younger son and affirm to him that regardless of his behavior, his identity as a son never changed. The father's words of affirmation are meant to speak rest and peace into the elder son's angry heart by communicating to him that hard work and obedience do not make him more accepted as a son. The father communicates to the sons that no separation exists between them. What belongs to the father belongs to the sons. They are family. They share everything. Whether at home with the father or away, obedient or disobedient, there is never a moment when both sons are not loved. Their father continually cherishes them as they both walk their paths, and while the two paths are very different, each leads them back home to their father's heart.

Jesus told this parable to reveal the character of God to us. Our God is diligent and persistent in His pursuit of relationship with us. He is an infinitely merciful Father who is not afraid to give us the freedom to walk away from fellowship with Him. Despite the pain He feels, He patiently waits while we ruin relationships, seek other gods, get our needs met though our own resources, and waste our time striving for an inheritance we already possess. His deepest desire is to bring His children home and welcome us back from distant lands without condemnation or punishment, with arms open wide, longing to bless. He showers us with affection, tells us who we are, and celebrates us. No matter what road we are on, the Father will come out to meet us and joyfully invite us to the party.

God's faithfulness to us does not change with our circumstances, and we need to understand how He is connected to us even during bad times. One of the primary ways God keeps His heart connected with ours is through compassion. When Scripture says Jesus was moved with compassion, the Greek word used, *splagchnizŏmai*, is packed with power and tenderness. It literally means His gut was wrenched with emotion when He encountered the pain of others. We see this when Jesus revealed the heart of His father through His love for society's outcasts.

In Jesus' time leprosy, an infectious disease causing severe, disfiguring skin sores, was deeply feared. Lepers were required to live outside the city and to yell "unclean" when anyone came close to them to prevent the infection from spreading. People ran from them and looked upon them with disgust. While others were shunning lepers, Jesus welcomed them. Not only was Jesus willing to be in the presence of the diseased, He was inclined to reach out and touch them. Those whom society feared and rejected, He embraced with compassion, kindness, and acceptance. Throughout the Gospel, Jesus showed the compassion of the Father. He mourned with His friends over the loss of a loved one. He felt the loneliness of the multitude who were without direction, the pains of the hungry, and the despair of the man hanging on the cross next to His.

> NO MATTER WHAT ROAD WE ARE ON, THE FATHER WILL COME OUT TO MEET US AND JOYFULLY INVITE US TO THE PARTY.

The Father's compassion for our suffering is boundless, regardless of whether we are experiencing pain due to no fault of our own or experiencing the fear and shame of being forced to face our sin head

CONCEPT OF GOD PART II

on. In John 4 and John 8, Jesus demonstrates compassion for two different women confronted with their own transgressions.

Although Jewish men typically avoided contact with Samaritans and women, the Scripture tells us in John 4 that Jesus chose to pass through Samaria and even engaged in conversation with a Samaritan woman who was desperately searching for love. She had been married five times and was currently living with a man who was not her husband. Jesus did not condemn her or try to heap guilt and shame on her. He revealed to her that she was fully known and fully loved in that moment, even in the midst of her sin. Jesus cared enough to confront her. He exposed the futility of the well she was trying to draw life from, but He did not leave her thirsty. He introduced His heart to hers in a way that caused her to know she was not alone and was deeply loved.

Not only are we fully known by God, we are fully loved as well. No matter how repetitive our attempts to find life outside of our relationship with God, our stubbornness does not prevent Him from seeking us out. He seeks us even when we are not seeking Him, and if we will simply let our thirst draw us to Him, we can finally end the cycles of pain we create for ourselves.

Battling shame is even harder when people are condemning us or we are condemning ourselves. In the eighth chapter of his gospel, John describes the encounter of a women caught in the act of adultery. She was brought before Jesus by the religious leaders. Can you imagine what this woman was feeling—the shame of public humiliation, the fear of facing her accusers alone, the terror of being escorted to her death? Jesus responded by addressing her accusers. He gave all of them the opportunity to prove themselves sinless, saying, "Let any of you who is without sin be the first to throw a stone at her" (John 8:7b). One by one her accusers walked away, leaving the woman with the only person in the world with the authority and righteousness to judge her. After Jesus pointed out that her accusers were no less sinful than she was, He released her from her shame, ensuring her He was for her, not condemning her. Her accusers judged her, put her at risk, made a spectacle of her, and used her as a tool in an attempt to bring about their own agenda. Revealing the heart of the Father, Jesus forgave, protected, and guided her, setting her free to walk in her forgiveness and leave her life of sin.

No matter how loud the voices of our accusers, whether they come from within or without, the voice of Love silences the critics and accepts us right where we are. God clears our hearts of shame and teaches us how to live. Motivated by His love, we can ignore the judgments of others, stop judging ourselves, walk away from our sin, and live free in Him.

But what about the times we don't just wander away from God, but rather turn our backs on Him? Most of us can easily relate to Peter, one of Jesus' disciples. His attitudes and actions were unpredictable and often got him into trouble. At times he was a passionate, devoted follower of Jesus while at other times his faith faltered. For example, Peter followed without hesitation when Jesus called him away from his profession of fishing. At Jesus' command, Peter courageously stepped out of the safety of a boat during a raging storm and walked on water. Peter boldly answered, "You are the Messiah, the Son of the living God," when Jesus asked Peter, "Who do you say that I am?" In response, Jesus proclaimed Peter to be a foundational stone of the church (Matthew 16:16-18). Peter professed a willingness to go to prison for Jesus and even die for Him. On the same night Jesus was arrested, Peter drew his sword and cut off the ear of one of the men trying to capture Jesus.

This same Peter, who had proclaimed his devotion with boldness, crumbled under the pressure of a horrific night. In fear at the questioning of others, he denied on three different occasions that he even knew Jesus, whom he had previously proclaimed to be the Messiah and declared he would go to prison and die for. Earlier in the day, Jesus had told Peter he would betray Jesus by denying Him three times before the rooster crowed in the morning. As Peter denied Jesus

NOT ONLY ARE WE FULLY KNOWN BY GOD, WE ARE FULLY LOVED AS WELL.

for the third time, his ears heard the rooster, and his eyes locked with the eyes of the one he had just betrayed. Imagine Peter's emotions. He looked into the eyes of Jesus, the one who perfectly loved him, after he had repeatedly forsaken Him. Devastated, Peter ran away weeping, abandoning the life Jesus had called him to, hiding in the familiarity of his previous occupation.

After the Resurrection, it would have been understandable if Jesus' attitude toward Peter had been disdainful. Jesus had every right to say Peter was no longer His friend or His brother and to repay betrayal with betrayal. Instead, Jesus reflected the heart of the Father, showing that even denying Him is not beyond God's mercy or His desire to share His love. Early one morning, after a night of fishing on the Sea of Galilee, Peter and his companions saw someone on the shore. One disciple recognized the person as Jesus. Peter's exuberance at seeing his friend and Savior alive on the shore would not allow him to wait for the boat to return. Peter jumped into the water and swam ashore. When he arrived on the beach, Peter did not find what we would expect, a critical, judgmental Jesus anxious to make retribution.

Instead, he found a forgiving, nurturing companion eager to restore relationship. Once the other disciples had arrived on the shore, Jesus invited them to share in a breakfast He had prepared for them over an open fire. After the meal, Jesus engaged Peter in an intimate conversation because He knew that for the sake of Peter's healing, Peter needed the opportunity to voice his devotion and once again embrace his calling (John 21:15-17).

We may have turned our backs on God. We may have even denied Him and run away. No matter how subtle or obvious our denial of God has been, our betrayal is not the end of the story. Breakfast is on the table. If we are willing to sit and eat, God is ready to sit and talk.

God is so powerful that He can create with the sound of His voice, yet He is so intimate that He invites us to call him Daddy or Papa. His pursuit of us is relentless. No matter where our aimless wandering takes us, no valley is deep enough, no crevice dark enough to hinder Him from finding us. He loves us enough to set us free to rest in His love or to strive to meet our needs elsewhere. As we wander through our lives, He patiently waits while His goodness woos us back to Him and joyfully celebrates us with passion upon our return. If we happen to find ourselves in a position of striving to earn what we already possess and judging those who are not performing according to our standards, He meets us in our loneliness and lovingly speaks rest into our exhausted, angry hearts.

While as humans, we are prone to run away from the forgotten, abandoned, and rejected, God moves in close. He is not afraid of our condition or repulsed by our circumstances. He is with us because He desires to be. He wants us just the way we are and not as society demands we should be. Even when our circumstances are a result of our own sin, He loves us enough to search us out. Our value to God isn't measured by our gender, race, or financial status. He doesn't value us less when we sin. His eyes are accepting, His arms are welcoming, and His heart is forgiving. He doesn't hold our past against us. He sets us free from that which binds us and affirms to us nothing can separate us from His love.

As our distorted views of His character dissolve and as the eyes of our hearts are opened to who He truly is, revelation replaces confusion. When our Concept of God grows and heals, grace floods our hearts. We stop striving so hard, begin to release our control, and slip into the contentment of a genuine and intimate relationship with God. Experiencing God for who He truly is has the power to change everything. Families that make up communities forgive each other more, communities that make up a society give more, and societies that make up a nation love and care more.

May you truly know Him, and may you stand in the light of His love and proclaim, "This is who my God is."

Prayer

You are not a hidden God. You have revealed Yourself in many ways, but none more descriptive than through Your beautiful Son. By revealing Your character through the life of Your Son, You give me the confidence to declare: You are Grace. You are Mercy. You are Compassion. You are Love. I allow the truth of Your character to awaken my soul and shape my life.

In Your Journal...

1. Taking into account the stories Jesus told and the way He interacted with people, what does Jesus communicate to us about the character of God?

2. Take a moment to meditate on the following promises of God:
   a. He will never abandon us (Hebrews 13:5).
   b. His love is unconditional and stronger than anything else that exists (Romans 8:38-39).
   c. He has promised to meet every need (Philippians 4:19).

4. How does each promise make you feel?

5. Describe how your life is going to change as the truth about God's character replaces the misconceptions discussed in the previous chapter.

Further Exercise

Imagine yourself having an intimate conversation with God. Be still, quiet your mind, and prepare yourself to listen to Him. Have someone read the following letter aloud to you, or if that is not possible, read it aloud to yourself, imagining each statement is being spoken by God directly to you.

Be still and listen so you can know me[A]. I want you to know me because knowing me is life[B]. I am so powerful I created the universe and everything in it through the sound of my voice[C], yet I am also so gentle you can find safety in my arms[D.] There is nothing about you I don't know[E]. I am keenly aware of even the smallest of details[F], and I accept you because I have made you acceptable[G]. My knowledge is not like human knowledge[H]. You can trust what I know over your narrow understanding[I]. Your vision is limited, but one day you will see clearly, as I do now[J].

Love is not just something I do; Love is who I am[K], and my love is designed to remove your fears[L]. Allow my love to quiet your mind, and listen as I sing over you[M]. You need my love, and my desire is to lavish my love on you[N]. My love for you never stops; it is everlasting because I am everlasting[O]. Absolutely nothing or no one can ever separate you from my love[P]. There is no way I will ever allow you to be pulled from my hands[Q].

I am close to you when your heart is breaking[R], I comfort you when you are troubled[S], and I promise I will never abandon you[T]. I will never stop being good to you[U]; everything that is good comes from me[V], and I am able to do more than you could ever imagine[W]. When you lie down at night, sleep in peace, knowing you are safe in me[X], and when you awaken in the morning, be aware of my mercies that are new every day[Y]. Even though you will have trouble in this world, you can take heart in knowing I have already overcome the troubles for you[Z]. May you allow my peace which passes all understanding to guard your heart and mind[AA], and may the eyes of your heart be enlightened so you may know who I truly am and all that you have in me[AB].

A. Psalm 46:10

B. John 17:3

C. Genesis 1:1-28

D. Isaiah 40:11

E. Psalm 139:1

F. Matthew 10:29-31

G. Ephesians 1:6

H. I Corinthians 1:25

I. Proverbs 3:5

J. I Corinthians 13:12

K. I John 4:8

L. I John 4:18

M. Zephaniah 3:17

N. I John 3:1

O. Jeremiah 31:3

P. Romans 8:38-39

Q. John 10:28

R. Psalm 34:18

S. II Corinthians 1:3-4

T. Hebrews 13:5

U. Jeremiah 32:40

V. James 1:17

W. Ephesians 3:20

X. Psalm 4:8

Y. Lamentations 3:22-23

Z. John 16:33

AA. Philippians 4:7

AB. Ephesians 1:18

CHAPTER EIGHT

WHAT'S THE VERDICT?

The True Word on Guilt

A TTEMPTING TO UNDERSTAND the role guilt plays in our lives can produce so much confusion that trying to manage our thoughts can feel like chasing ping pong balls in a wind tunnel. Do we always deserve to feel the guilt we are feeling? What about times when we don't feel the emotion of guilt even though the situation seems to call for it? Guilt can be both a concrete fact as well as an emotion we feel. How do we make sense of a topic that is both objective and subjective?

Misunderstood and unresolved guilt have the potential to stunt our growth, wear us down, and kill any meaningful relationship. The wide spectrum of guilt means it can affect each of us differently. For some, guilt can be a mild, constant, nagging voice, while for others, it can cripple or even paralyze our souls. How we learn to manage guilt as children follows us into adulthood and has a direct effect on our level of peace. Whether we've learned to ignore the guilt or wallow in it, trying to manage guilt through our own methods leaves us in unresolved pride or pain.

To understand the relevance of guilt in our lives, we need to recognize the difference between false and true guilt. False guilt is produced by an overgrown conscience, often developed by unhealthiness and dysfunction within our family and cultural systems. We experience false guilt when we think we are accountable for actions, people, situations, or events that are not truly our responsibility. By contrast, feelings of true guilt are produced by behavior that contradicts how God designed us to live. We experience true guilt when the Holy Spirit shines a light on behaviors that hurt others or ourselves.

Katelyn, the oldest of four siblings, was forced to be responsible for her brothers and sister beginning when she was only eight years old. Her parents would often go out and socialize with their friends, leaving Katelyn to take care of the other children and putting pressure on her no child is ever designed to feel. As an adult, Katelyn struggled with a warped sense of responsibility. She felt guilty when the people around her struggled or failed. She also felt guilty whenever she had to say no to a request. However, once Katelyn experienced healing concerning how her false guilt resulted from her family's dysfunction, this false guilt no longer controlled her. After healing, she no longer believed she was responsible for other people, and she was able to tell herself the truth in situations where false guilt previously would have controlled her. Katelyn now has a life of freedom she never imagined was possible.

While Katelyn felt false guilt she was never designed to feel throughout much of her childhood and early adulthood, her parents avoided confronting their own, true guilt. From time to time, the Holy Spirit would begin to convict Katelyn's parents for making her feel responsible for her siblings. Instead of listening to the guilt and allowing it to create the change God wanted for the family, her parents would make excuses such as, "Our lives are so busy. We need Katelyn to be responsible for the younger kids on the weekends so we can have a break." Years of ignoring and suppressing the guilt began to affect Katelyn's parents in many negative ways, including depression and anxiety. They were saddened by the wall between them and their eldest daughter. Once they finally faced the true guilt, they were able to find relief and begin to restore their relationship with Katelyn.

While false guilt is a feeling we want gone from our lives, true guilt should be embraced. True guilt is the feeling of regret we experience when we violate the inner principles and values God has written on our hearts and in our consciences. Even though talking about guilt in a positive light is difficult, true guilt does have a purpose in our lives. It lets us know when we are hurting ourselves and others. If we learn to listen, as Katelyn's parents eventually did, true guilt will help us make peace where there is conflict, and it will protect us from making the same mistakes over and over again. The damage comes when we refuse to listen to it or when we allow guilt to linger and never become resolved. If we ignore our guilt, we will go through life continually hurting ourselves and others, never experiencing the freedom that guilt is designed to urge us toward. We will find ourselves overly defensive, unwilling to listen to the healthy criticism necessary for growth.

While Katelyn's parents were faced with unresolved true guilt, our emotions can be affected by any lingering guilt in our lives, whether true or false. This lingering guilt can lead to shame, which we will address in the next chapter. Additionally, we may find ourselves dealing with depression or anxiety. We may feel lonely or become so overwhelmed we feel hopeless. Some of us may experience constant fear. Unresolved guilt can also turn into anger, which simmers below the surface until we can no longer control it and lash out verbally or physically. Living this way for long periods of time, we may become emotionally exhausted or even numb.

When we live with unresolved guilt, our behavior can be affected as much as our emotions. We may suffer from addiction, isolate ourselves from others, or engage in other behaviors intended to prevent us from getting hurt. We might become critical or judgmental of ourselves or others, constantly raising the bar and creating new hoops to jump through. Other times, performing or overachieving can become our focus. Codependent relationships are very common when we have unresolved guilt. We also might attempt to "balance the scales" by obsessing over repaying or

IF WE IGNORE OUR GUILT, WE WILL GO THROUGH LIFE CONTINUALLY HURTING OURSELVES AND OTHERS, NEVER EXPERIENCING THE FREEDOM THAT GUILT IS DESIGNED TO URGE US TOWARD

making up for mistakes instead of resting in the grace of the cross and making amends to those we've hurt when the timing is right. Other common ways of dealing with guilt include minimizing our own sin or shifting the blame onto others. All of these behaviors can not only have a negative impact on our lives, but also become so engrained we don't even realize what we're doing or why we're doing it. Until we process through the guilt that haunts us, our emotions will remain out of balance and our behavior will reflect those emotions.

When it comes to guilt, we cannot possibly get through this life without ever facing it. We have all sinned; we have all fallen short of who we were truly created to be, walking in union with God, dependent on Him for life and love. We have all taken our lives into our own hands. Even though we may never actually voice the words, our attempts to control ourselves, others, and circumstances declare loudly, "My trust is in myself."

In the end, our control and sin always leave us feeling the same—confused, frustrated, trapped, empty, sad, and guilty. Our walls become tall and strong as we attempt to stay in control. All of our relationships bear the mark of our sins. While those we are in conflict with have their issues as well, we must see **we** are the common denominator in all of these relational issues.

When it comes to our relationship with God, although He is right where He has always been, our guilt-ridden perception lies to us and tells us our past is a wall standing between us and Him. In truth, He is using our past as a bridge. God does not see our past the way we do. We see it as a hindrance; He sees it as an opportunity. He patiently waits for us to navigate around our guilt by our own methods until we finally stumble our way to the relief found at the cross.

On our journey to the cross, guilt is not the only emotion we must face. Fear is a powerful emotion accompanying guilt. Every act of control is fear motivated. We desperately need the transformation that comes when fear is removed from our daily inventory of forces to deal with. It is common to think the solution to fear is courage; however, there is a force greater than courage that drives fear away: Love (I John 4:18).

The loving arms of God can squeeze so tightly that fear and guilt have no room to breathe and therefore no longer have a constant place in our lives. In that space of love, we feel free to be ourselves with no need to put on the false self. There is no greater reality to grasp than this: You are deeply loved.

While love is the greatest force in the universe, it is meaningless unless it is expressed. The most powerful expressions of love are seen through ultimate sacrifice, when love is demonstrated through the willingness of one person to lay down their life for another. God chose to express His love for us in a way that would change how love is viewed throughout history.

Even before the beginning of time, our Father, Jesus, and the Holy Spirit envisioned an event so passionate They knew it would touch the deepest places of our hearts. This event is a timeless expression of love that has created a sacred space for us to be drawn into and allow love to remove all guilt and ease all fears. The cross is the place where God left our sin and where death was abolished. The death and resurrection of Jesus provide the pathway to the freedom, peace, and wholeness we all desire. Jesus said, "I am the way, and the truth, and the life" (John 14:6). We need a way because we are lost. We need the truth because we are contaminated by lies. We need life because the end result of our sins is death.

THERE IS NO GREATER REALITY TO GRASP THAN THIS: YOU ARE DEEPLY LOVED.

We experience a wide range of severities of death as a result of sin. Eternally speaking, sin produced a death that would have left us forever separated from the life of God. Thankfully, the aggressive grace of God refused to let sin and death have the last word. Where once we were separated, we now have been brought back together. God was and is in Christ, reconciling the world back to Himself (II Corinthians 5:19). We find a safe place in knowing death has been conquered, and even though one day our physical bodies will stop functioning, our true selves will never die.

While the system of sin and death has been settled eternally, we still deal with the principle daily on a smaller scale. With each attempt to exert control, we die a little. The deaths we experience can take on many different forms, including the deaths of relationships or inner peace. Regardless of their form, they all lead to constant dead ends and destructive results in our lives.

Guilt and fear keep the cycle of death and destruction in motion. We tell ourselves we are guilty and go through cycles from living like a guilty person to trying to muster enough pride or denial to make the guilt go away. This leads us to a place of utter hopelessness until we hear the voice of liberation declare that He has made us innocent.

Imagine you commit a crime and are so afraid of punishment that you go on the run. For years, you are living a lie, trying your best to forget what you did, but knowing deep down, you did something wrong and it's going to catch up to you one day. Sometimes you are able to ignore the guilt inside you so thoroughly you can almost forget about it; other times, the guilt becomes so overwhelming you can barely stand the pressure. You may have tried to start over and be a good person, but you're slowly being crushed by the weight of the crime you committed. Now imagine, after years of guilt and shame, of hiding the truth from yourself and everyone around you, that you open up the newspaper one morning to find out the judge has dismissed your case and all the charges against you have been dropped. As you continue reading, you discover that even before the world began, an agreement of love was made to ensure your security. Someone willingly agreed to stand in your place, and by His sacrifice, you have been set free. Imagine the radical change in your life as you receive the truth that you can stop running. Trying to manage or ignore your guilt is no longer a part of your thinking because you can rest in the gift of your verdict: **not guilty**.

For so many of us, this story is not far-fetched. Either we have not heard the verdict of innocence, or we have heard yet forgotten it. We are running scared, hiding behind pride, allowing our guilt and fear to govern our souls. Yet in Colossians 2:14, we find we no longer have to be crushed by guilt over our sins. God has already forgiven us. He has taken everything against us—the list of charges, the evidence, the eyewitness statements, the verdict, the sentence—and nailed it to the cross. He has wiped it all away.

> YOUR LIST OF SINS HAD ITS PLACE FIXED BETWEEN THE HARD WOOD OF THE CROSS AND THE SOFT HAND OF YOUR BROTHER, YOUR SAVIOR.

Oftentimes, when we think of the cross, we picture a symbol found decorating churches and hanging from necklaces. Unfortunately, the cross itself becomes our focal point instead of who sacrificed Himself on it. When we think of the One who died for us, we should try to avoid picturing just a statue or a symbol of Jesus hanging on the cross. He is not a mere symbol. He is real, and He is family. He is our Brother because we share the same Father (Hebrews 2:11). Become aware of and rest in what's been done for you. Claim what has always been declared. You are innocent. You are free. You are forgiven. No matter what your past may attempt to tell you, this is **who you are**. Your sins have been separated from you as far as the east is from the west (Psalm 103:12), so they do not identify you.

Looking back to Chapter 4, we find the list of our false selves' behaviors, which are our methods of control. Some of these behaviors are easier to recognize as sins than others, such as adultery, lying, and violence, while examples such as passivity, busyness, and self-righteousness are often ignored. However, they are all sin because they come from a place of fear and control. No one's behavior is sinless. We have all sinned. We have all missed the mark. We have all attempted to control. And we've all suffered the conflict and frustration resulting from our sins.

Your list of sins had its place fixed between the hard wood of the cross and the soft hand of your Brother, your Savior. His blood has dissolved your list forever. God has taken your list out of the way. He was not going to allow it to stand between you and Him. So for God's sake, and your own, don't allow it to stand between you and peace.

May you claim your verdict of innocence as you rest in God's sacrificial love, and may you walk in the victory of a resurrected life.

PRAYER

Father, teach me to embrace the perfect purpose that true guilt plays in my life. Use my guilt to open my eyes to the sacrificial love of the cross and the victory of the empty tomb. I receive Your ultimate expression of love, where my guilt has been resolved. I rest in my forgiveness. I receive my innocence. I gaze at the cross with humility, and with a heart of gratitude say thank you for the gift of redemption. Amen.

IN YOUR JOURNAL...

1. What is the difference between true and false guilt?

2. Why is experiencing true guilt in a healthy way important?

3. Why is recognizing false guilt important?

4. In what ways has unresolved guilt affected your life?

5. If reading about God's expression of love through the cross makes you feel grateful, write a prayer to Him expressing your gratitude for resolving your guilt and declaring you innocent. Create some sacred space to read the prayer out loud to God.

FURTHER EXERCISES

Take some time to think about the areas of your life where you often feel false guilt. List the thoughts driving this false guilt. For example: "It's my job to make everyone else happy. If I say no to a request, I am not a loving person."

Then write down and meditate on the truth in response to each lie. For example: "It is not my job to please everyone else at the expense of my own peace. Saying no can be healthy."

Next, take some time and meditate on the areas in your life in which you have felt true guilt.

Make a list of your sins using the following prompts. Refer back to the false self list from Chapter 4 if necessary:

What do you feel true guilt about?
What have you done to hurt yourself?
What have you done that has hurt others?
What have you done that was not in harmony with how God designed you to live?

Pray through the items on your list one by one, thanking God for His forgiveness given through the death of His Son, Jesus. Place all your trust in the finished work of Jesus and rest in your innocence.

CHAPTER NINE

IDENTITY

Meet the Real You

*W*HEN OUR FALSE SELF IS EXPOSED for what it is and we take the leap of faith of declaring, **"My false self is *not* who I am,"** we are left with a question that can cause us a great deal of fear. "If my false self is not who I am, then who am I?" *Who am I?* is a question leading to life-changing revelation if answered by the One who knows who we truly are.

Imagine a family is camping deep in the woods, far away from civilization. One member of the family, a small toddler, gets lost and somehow miraculously learns how to survive on his own. He spends the next thirty years alone, living off the land. One day, hunters come across him and ask him who he is. Naturally, having no recollection of his parents, or any other human for that matter, he does not understand what the hunters are asking him. The man is taken to the hospital in a nearby town, where a group of doctors, social workers, and teachers all work with him to help him assimilate into society. After several months of learning, the man is asked once again, "Who are you?" Even though he now understands the question, because he has no memory of belonging to anyone, his answer is, "I don't know who I am."

A few days later, while watching the local news, the man's father sees the report and realizes his son has been found. When the father arrives where his son is being held, he embraces his long-lost child and claims him, spending the next few hours telling him who he is. As the two are leaving the hospital to return home, a reporter asks the son, "Who are you?" Now, finally, he has an answer: "I am his son, he is my father, and I belong to a family." The son did not know his identity until someone other than himself told him who he was.

We are no different. We must have someone other than ourselves tell us who we are. The problem is we allow all the wrong people to answer this sacred question: Who am I?

As human beings, we are a special creation of God's. We are His workmanship (Ephesians 2:10). The Greek word for workmanship is poiema, from which we get the word poem. We are His creation, His work of art. Not only do we bear His story; we also bear His image. We have an honor and dignity no other part of creation can claim. We are created in the image of our Creator (Genesis 1:26).

Let us use Charles Boyer's brilliant lithograph of Mickey Mouse's self-portrait as an illustration of a life-changing message. In this work of art, we find Mickey painting a self-portrait by looking at himself in a mirror. The image we see in the mirror is Mickey. However the image Mickey sees, the same image he paints on the canvas, is none other than his creator, Walt Disney himself.

The next time you look in a mirror, look deep into your own eyes and notice what you see. Do you see shame? Insecurities? Arrogance? Or do you see the reflection of your Creator? It is time for us to give ourselves and others the dignity our Creator gives us. When He made us, He declared, "It is good." Let us declare the same. Nothing created in His image warrants the depreciating, demeaning attitude we give ourselves and others.

Judging ourselves is an endless cycle of pain. We have been declared innocent from any and all condemning charges. Our Father proclaims that no person or system can hold anything against His children. Even though we still need the emotion of guilt that teaches, protects, and corrects us when we've done something our Father knows will hurt us, we are free from the oppression of crippling shame and the paralysis resulting from our fear of punishment.

WE MUST HAVE SOMEONE OTHER THAN OURSELVES TELL US WHO WE ARE.

While guilt and shame can seem to be the same, there are differences. Guilt addresses our behavior and is designed to cause us to look at what we've done. Shame, on the other hand, is an emotion that points to our identity rather than our behavior. Shame is the smoke leading us back to the fire of the lies we believe about ourselves. When we experience shame, we have the opportunity to cooperate with God in rooting out the lies and receiving the revelation of truth concerning who we are in Him.

We are His children, and even though He has set us free to engage the pain and suffering of life, we are promised we will never be alone and will always belong to Him. He is an attentive Father, and together with Christ and the Holy Spirit, we belong to an ever-present family. He intimately likes us and enjoys our company. He is a Father who is always available, never too busy, never distracted. His presence is not a mere visitation, but an inhabitation. He has permanently set up residence, and we find Him and our true selves resting in the home He has built inside of us. This home is a safe one, and by the sacrifice of our Brother, Jesus, we have the peace of knowing the war has been won. We will never have to fear being lost to the enemy that is death.

While a part of us is still in process, at our core, no work is needed. In the depths of our true selves, we are complete; we are whole. We already are everything our false selves are trying to become. As Watchman Nee said in *The Normal Christian Life*, "Think of the bewilderment of trying to get into a room in which you already are!" We already belong. We already are deeply loved and valued. We have a safe place set in His heart, and He holds us cradled in His hands. Once in His hands, we are promised we will never be snatched away by anyone (John 10:28).

YOU ARE COMPLETE.

YOU ARE WHOLE.

YOU ARE RIGHTEOUS.

YOU ARE REDEEMED.

No matter how intense or distressful the days may be, nothing can change the fact we are the children of the Creator and our Brother is King of the Kingdom in which we stand victorious. Our confidence comes from being a part of a family of victory. We cannot lose because we have already won. We have inherited a conquering identity and nothing that comes against us can succeed.

Imagine feeling so secure in our identities we no longer look to anyone or anything from the outside to tell us who we are. Our critics' voices are silenced, and our names from the past no longer haunt us. While we will still have a keen awareness when stung by rejection, even though we feel hurt, the rejection no longer has the power to define us ever again. We will no longer feel the need to compare ourselves with others, becoming discontent with ourselves, because we are satisfied with who we are. When we do make mistakes, we are a gentle friend to ourselves, forgiving with a heart of mercy because we cherish the wonderfulness of who God has made us to be.

Instead of striving to gain status, we realize we can rest and function from a position already attained for us. Life becomes a lot less about becoming and more about simply being. The way we manage expectations drastically changes because we are no longer performing for ourselves, others, or God. The common pressures of a faulty system of expectations lift as we walk in the ease of grace and rest in the arms of Love.

We no longer assign the same value to the things and goals we used to. We view our careers, churches, family, friends, and even our hobbies through a different lens. Nothing and no one has the power to tell us who we are except our Creator, Savior, Lover, and Life. There is no room for the ego boost of pride and arrogance because the insecurities we fear are replaced and our deficits are replenished.

As God's beloved children, we have the same spiritual DNA. We find unity in knowing that together, we share family names; we are Complete, Whole, Righteous, and Redeemed. When we embrace our identities together, we walk with an attitude of dignity and confidence, seeing ourselves united as a family, and we cease to focus on what divides us, cherishing instead the bond that holds us all together.

While these family names can help us to come together with others and be secure in our place within the whole, we also must not forget the whole is made up of individuals, and each of us is unique. Even as an individual, the same names still apply. You still possess the same dignity and worth from being a child of God. You are complete. You are whole. You are righteous. You are redeemed.

But on an even deeper level, God wants us to discover and embrace certain specific names to replace the old lies that have been removed. Our beliefs about ourselves are so crucial that they cannot be over emphasized. Whether consciously or subconsciously, the names we've adopted from our wounds are what set the course for our lives. Our thoughts flow from our beliefs, our emotions are spurred on by our beliefs, and our actions are manifestations of what we believe. These beliefs remain stored in the soul until they are replaced. Embracing our new names results in transformation by the renewing of our minds (Romans 12:1).

The common question that arises is this: If I am everything God says I am, why do I still struggle with sin? The answer is complex. While it's true that at our core, our identities are settled and sealed for all eternity, there is yet a part of us in the process of becoming what our core already is. That part is our character. Our character is where the refining work is being done. It is moldable, changeable; it is becoming. Theology refers to this as the process of sanctification.

One primary tool God uses to sanctify or refine our character is pain. As we experience difficulties, we have an opportunity to grow because the defects in our character come out under pressure. Time plus pressure reveal the parts of our character that have not yet been transformed. As we cooperate with God in our pain, we allow Him to shape our character into one of peace and trust. The more trials we go through, the more we become accustomed to the sanctification process and its beauty. We can always know our pain is not wasted (Romans 5:1-5).

While we should be aware of the development of our character, peace is found as we allow our focus to rest on the finished work at the core of our identity. At our core, we are whole, as our character is being made whole. We are righteous, as our character is being made righteous. We are pure at our core, as our character is being purified. We are free, as we are being made free. At our core, we are complete, as our character is being made complete. We are at peace, as our character is discovering peace. At our core, we are love, as our character is becoming more loving.

Trust is not stagnant, and we are not called to be passive in our growth. With our free will, we have the opportunity to allow pain and love to have their place in our experience. We declare our trust in the Shaper of our character through brokenness and obedience.

WE HAVE DAMAGED THE WORLD BECAUSE WE HAVE DAMAGED OURSELVES, AND WE HAVE DAMAGED OURSELVES BECAUSE WE DON'T KNOW WHO WE ARE.

Jesus said, "Come to me, all you who are weary and burdened, and I will give you rest. Take my yoke upon you and learn from me, for I am gentle and humble in heart, and you will find rest for your souls. For my yoke is easy, and my burden is light" (Matthew 11:28-30). Rest. Easy. Light. We experience these as we become more aware of who we are in Christ and begin to identify ourselves with Him. When we yoke ourselves to Him, we set our minds on what already is and with trust, surrender the parts of ourselves that are still becoming.

We don't have to look very hard to see we still carry the fallen part of humanity somewhere inside us. Our selfish attitudes and actions confirm we are not living according to the original design. We feel it.

We know it. We have damaged the world because we have damaged ourselves, and we have damaged ourselves because we don't know who we are. We didn't start the destruction. It has been a part of the world since the first act of disobedience in the Garden with Adam and Eve, trickling down through all generations. We feel so far removed from who we were designed to be that recovery sometimes seems hopeless. But all is not hopeless; when we see ourselves for who we truly are, we discover hope is part of the fabric of our being.

We often make the mistake of looking in the mirror, seeing the reflection of our outer parts, and stopping there. We look at our bodies and try to fix what we're critical of, while maximizing what we think is going well for us. Fortunately, the truth is we are so much more than just our physical bodies.

> WE EMPHASIZE HIM WHILE HE EMPHASIZES US BECAUSE THAT'S HOW HEALTHY, INTIMATE RELATIONSHIPS WORK.

If we believe in an afterlife, we believe that we, our true selves, go on living after our bodies die. When our bodies die, we don't. Therefore, our true identities are more spiritual than physical. Pierre Teilhard de Chardin has expressed this truth as, "We are spiritual beings having a human experience." In order for us to realize who we truly are, we must first embrace the truth that we are spiritual beings.

Sadly, the term "born again" comes with so much political, cultural, and religious baggage. The new birth is a beautiful way to describe our spiritual formation. In Jesus' conversation with Nicodemus, He makes it a point to separate the two births: "That which is born of the flesh is flesh, and that which is born of the Spirit is spirit" (John 3:6). Jesus wanted Nicodemus to see there is a spiritual birth that takes place, and this new birth gives us the spiritual eyes to see the Kingdom of God and the capacity to enter it. We are awakened by a life that is eternal.

We possess eternal life, but what does that mean? "Eternal" is an adjective describing the noun "life." When we think of the word eternal, we think of ideas such as never-ending and forever. These definitions are close to the truth but incomplete. Eternal means never ending, but it also means never beginning. So when we possess eternal life, we possess the only life with no beginning and no ending, God's life.

While the eternal life within us does include the entire Trinity, Father, Son, and Holy Spirit, so much of the New Testament seems to single out Christ as the focal point. In Colossians 1:26-27, Paul refers to the presence of Christ within us as a mystery that has been revealed: "the mystery that has been kept hidden for ages and generations, but is now disclosed to the saints. To them God has chosen to make known among the Gentiles the glorious riches of this mystery, which is Christ in you, the hope of glory." Before Jesus, God shut mouths and used silence to keep the mystery a secret. However, we are blessed to live in an age when we have the opportunity to allow the secret to break out of its silence and manifest itself in our awareness, changing our lives forever.

The indwelling life of Christ makes us who we are. We are in Him and He is in us. His Spirit has joined with our spirit and we are one (I Corinthians 6:17). Being placed into Him gives us the totality of Him and His life. In Christ we find a sinless existence, a redeeming crucifixion, a victorious resurrection, and a never-ending relationship that death cannot touch. Being made one with Him in our spirits, our old identities have been crucified. We have been spiritually resurrected from the dead, being made new creatures fashioned in victory. And through all eternity, nothing can separate us from Him and His love because we are in Him. As the mystery of Christ within us begins to be revealed, we become aware of a permanent fusion. We have everything He has, and we are everything He is.

This has nothing to do with us, and yet it has everything to do with us. We do not work for, earn, achieve, or accomplish who we are. His life, His work, His love, and His acceptance put our focus on Him, yet by grace, He chooses us, redeems us, makes us new. He loves us, adores us, and values us. We emphasize Him while He emphasizes us because that's how healthy, intimate relationships work.

He has made you pure, complete, whole, redeemed, rescued, righteous, free. This is the truth. Therefore, the distorted beliefs about yourself that have been causing you pain must be lies. They cannot be true, no matter how much they "feel" true. As the truth is revealed to you, the lies will not feel true anymore.

From this day forward, God is the only one who has your permission to tell you who you are. As His affirming voice becomes clearer, may your experiences of peace become more frequent. While there are still occasional fears to be calmed, pains to be experienced, and rejections to be felt, these define you no more—because they never did. From now on, you will be able to accept the process your character is in because you know the truth of who you are at your core.

May you experience your true self as you see your reflection in the eyes of your Creator, and may you rest in knowing that you already are all you have been striving to become.

Prayer

Father, from this day forward, I give You and You alone permission to tell me who I am. I receive Your truth and allow the revelation of who I am to drive out every lie I have believed about myself. Silence my inner critic and let every lie spoken to me bounce off my ears and disintegrate into the air. I receive my true identity in Christ. His death was my death, His resurrection is my resurrection, and at this very moment, we are all eternally one. Amen.

In Your Journal...

1. How has your life been affected by the lies you believe about yourself?

2. Describe how your relationship with yourself is going to change as you receive and rest in your true identity in Christ.

3. Read the following list of "Who I Am" statements silently. After you've read it once, read it again, aloud to yourself and God, claiming your true identity. Refer to this list as often as necessary for the rest of your life.

Who Am I?

I Corinthians 6:17	I am one spirit with God
Acts 17:29	I am God's offspring
I John 3:6	I am God's child
I John 5:18	I am born of God and the evil one cannot touch me
Ephesians 2:4-5	I am loved
Romans 8:37-39	I am safe in the love of God
Colossians 1:14	I am redeemed by the blood of Jesus
John 15:15	I am Christ's friend
Romans 8:1	I am free from condemnation
Hebrews 10:14	I am perfect in Christ
Romans 5:19	I am righteous
Ephesians 2:10	I am God's workmanship
Ephesians 1:4	I am chosen
Ephesians 1:4	I am holy and blameless
II Corinthians 5:17	I am a new creation
Hebrews 13:5	I am not alone
Galatians 5:1	I am free
II Corinthians 5:21	I am righteous
John 10:28	I am safe

FURTHER EXERCISES

1. Make a list of all your "I am" lies. For example, I'm not good enough, I'm dirty, I'm worthless.

2. Renounce the lies out loud, one by one. This may take the form of a statement such as, "I renounce the lie that I am worthless, in Jesus' name."

3. Destroy the list.

4. Claim the truth aloud using the "Who Am I?" list above. This may take the form of a statement such as, "I claim the truth that I am free, in Jesus' name."

Chapter Ten

Forgiveness

It's What We Do Because It's Who We Are

W E KNOW ALL THE CLICHÉS about refusing to forgive someone who has wronged us. It is like drinking poison and expecting the other person to die. It's like setting yourself on fire and
hoping the other person dies of smoke inhalation. We know holding on
to bitterness and offenses is only hurting us, so why do we do it? The
answer is simple and not a mystery at all. We are hesitant to forgive
because unforgiveness seems to have benefits. We have been deceived
into believing that holding on to offenses serves us.

Letting go of attitudes that seem to produce the emotions we are
chasing is difficult. While our true self wants to relinquish control
and be set free, our false self wants to stay in control. The false self
clenches and hangs on to unforgiveness because when we hold on to an
offense, we feel like we have the power. Unforgiveness gives us a false
sense of superiority to those who hurt us. The lie we believe is, "If I
forgive them, they win." Unforgiveness allows us to stay in a posture
of judgment. We are the judge, the offender is the criminal, we are in
control, and they need to be punished. We hold on to the offense as a

form of punishment. Unforgiveness gives us a sense of entitlement. As long as somebody owes us, we will never be broke.

Another reason we avoid forgiveness is that anger feels better than pain, and we know intuitively if we give up our anger, we will have to face the hurt hiding behind it. The bigger the offense is, the deeper the hurt and the more impossible it seems to forgive. Yet these deep wounds and the pain they cause are what fuel our false selves. We do everything we can to run from the pain, bury it, ignore it, minimize it, medicate it, counteract it, instead of facing it and forgiving the initial offense. We become so comfortable with our current attitudes and behaviors that we need someone to keep blaming so we can keep functioning through our false selves. We know if we forgive that our excuses for our present attitudes and behaviors will be stripped away.

> **WE KNOW IF WE FORGIVE THAT OUR EXCUSES FOR OUR PRESENT ATTITUDES AND BEHAVIORS WILL BE STRIPPED AWAY.**

Neurological studies have even shown that when we fixate on repaying those who've wronged us, the pleasure pathways in our brains light up, according to clinical psychologist Dr. Everett Worthington. In the 2007 documentary The Power of Forgiveness, he discusses how unforgiveness actually produces a high we learn to chase. Even as our souls are desperately seeking peace, our brains crave revenge.

Unforgiveness is a powerful weapon we learn to find safety in wielding. Laying that weapon down leaves us feeling exposed and vulnerable, but this is the only way you can truly know yourself and be truly known by others.

What causes us to finally entertain the idea of laying our weapons down? Until the pain of staying the same exceeds the pain of change, there is no change. Even when we recognize the misery and hurt inside us, sometimes the pain still isn't bad enough that we are willing to make the changes necessary to find lasting relief and peace.

While unforgiveness seems to have benefits, they are an illusion that can lead to damaging and painful consequences if we continue to hold on to our offenses. Meaningful relationships are difficult while holding on to unforgiveness. We can end up hurting others the way we were hurt. We can also use indifference to keep others at a distance or find ourselves easily irritated over trivial things, continually running from the real problems, real pain, and real pressures.

Some of us escape the pain by trying to create the perfect world and placing our heads in the sand. We've learned how to "fake it until we make it." We find ourselves escaping reality by rationalizing and making excuses, smiling when we're hurting, and laughing when nothing is funny. The depression that comes from our unresolved offenses is no laughing matter. Frequently sighing, difficulty sleeping, or escaping into sleep are common. Grinding teeth, especially at night, as well as other jaw problems, headaches, and soreness in the upper back and neck can all come from the tension of storing our pain when we need to release it. Our critical, negative attitude creates a black hole of discomfort, emotionally, mentally, and sometimes even physically. When things finally get bad enough, we entertain the thought of forgiving.

As our hearts are in the process of preparing to forgive, we can encounter many stumbling blocks and points of confusion. For example, many people incorrectly assume forgiveness should always lead to reconciliation. If we desire a free heart, forgiveness is a must; however, reconciling the relationship with the person whom we are forgiving is not always healthy. Some relationships are simply toxic, and establishing healthy boundaries may be necessary.

Maria suffered abuse from a controlling boyfriend for years. After the relationship ended, she made the crucial step of reaching out for help because her ex kept trying to win her back and she was dealing with conflicting emotions. Around four months into the counseling process, the time came for Maria to forgive her ex-boyfriend. A tremendous fear rose up within Maria because she was confusing forgiveness with reconciliation. She assumed if she forgave her ex, God would then expect her to reestablish a relationship with him. Maria was deeply relieved when she realized she could experience the freedom of fully forgiving her ex while at the same time God was calling her to cut all ties and end all communication with him.

Even though reconciliation is not always a good idea, we shouldn't use this as an excuse not to have a relationship with someone who is not a threat to us. God is in the business of reconciliation, and as His children, we are called to the same. As Paul writes in Romans 12:18, "If it is possible, as far as it depends on you, live at peace with everyone."

Ever since they were children, Jack has had conflict with his older sister, who has a dominant attitude. Her constant attempts to control family situations have left Jack feeling bitter toward her. Jack finally grew weary of the bitterness and decided to forgive his sister. After praying through all the anger and forgiving his sister in his heart, Jack began to sense God calling him to meet with her and have a conversation. Jack had attempted to repair their relationship in the past, all with no result. However since he now had forgiven her and stopped judging her, he knew their next conversation would have a completely different feel to it. For a few days, Jack resisted contacting her to set up a meeting time. His fear and pride welled up, and he found himself thinking, "Just because I have forgiven her doesn't mean I have to have a relationship with her." While this statement is true, Jack was hiding behind this way of thinking because he was afraid of his sister's reaction to the conversation and because he didn't know what a close relationship with her would look like. After realizing that reengaging his sister was the unavoidable next step God was leading him toward, Jack recognized his fearful and prideful false self, and asked her to lunch. This was the first step in reconciliation.

In addition to confusing forgiveness with reconciliation, other stumbling blocks can arise when certain actions or situations fool us into believing we have already forgiven the other person when we really haven't. Sometimes we believe we have already experienced forgiveness just because we no longer feel anger or hatred towards them. We may have taken the time to put ourselves in their shoes and attempt to understand why they did that to us, or separate the person from their behavior. Possibly, we have even taken the opportunity to confront our offender or attempt reconciliation with them.

If enough time has passed, we may tell ourselves, "Time heals all wounds," or "It was so long ago that it doesn't really matter anymore." Time and distance can cause us to believe what happened was not really a big deal, especially if we rarely think about the offender or what they did. We may already be willing to be nice to the other person, to try to forget about what happened, or act like it never happened at all. Perhaps we have even prayed for the other person and asked God to forgive them.

However, just because we have asked God to forgive someone who has hurt us doesn't mean that *we* have forgiven them. All of the actions described above can create the *illusion* of forgiveness, but none of them are the *same* as forgiveness. Until we have truly forgiven and released them, either we will continue to harbor the exhausting anger and nagging bitterness poisoning our lives or else we will just go numb. When we are numb or emotionally shut down, we are missing out on life. We can't choose which emotions we want to feel and which ones we don't. Stuff one emotion down and we stuff them all until the only one left is the secondary emotion of anger.

As our emotions are awakened and brought into balance, we will find ourselves capable of feeling the emotion that allows us to relate to God on a deep level, compassion. Compassion is connected to forgiveness in the sense that one will follow the other, but in no particular order. Compassion can come before forgiveness, paving the way, or it can be a by-product of forgiveness. Without compassion, there is no forgiveness, and vice-versa. However, it's also important to let them stand alone because one does not equal the other. Compassion comes from the Latin *compati*, meaning "to suffer with." At some point, you must allow yourself to suffer with the one who wounded you. What is their pain? What is their story? What are their wounds? Who hurt them? Having compassion for those who hurt us can be extremely difficult but is necessary if we desire peace in our own hearts.

In Chapter 8, we discussed how God has forgiven us for our sins, how He took everything that was against us and nailed it to the cross. We no longer have to feel the crushing weight of guilt and shame that comes from the list of sins hanging over our heads. We have been set free. And just as God has forgiven us, He grants us the opportunity to forgive others. Even though we have been released from the weight of our sins, we cannot truly be free if we still live with bitterness and anger against those who have wronged us.

We are forgiving the other person not only for what they did but also for the lies created because of their offense, the emotions that we felt, and our behavior and attitudes formed because of the lies. The aftermath of a disaster can be as emotionally devastating for those affected as the event itself. Similarly, when someone else wrongs us, the lies formed because of our wounds, and the choices we make out of our woundedness, can sometimes have as much of a negative effect on us as the initial offense. When we forgive another person for wronging us, we must forgive them totally and completely, not just for what they did, but for all the results of their actions, even if those results came about through our choices and not theirs. Without out total forgiveness for an offense and its results, we often continue to follow the same path we began in our woundedness because we still believe the same lies.

AT SOME POINT, YOU MUST ALLOW YOURSELF TO SUFFER WITH THE ONE WHO WOUNDED YOU.

In our pursuit of total forgiveness, we may be faced with the challenge of forgiving someone who has departed this life. Because the other person is gone, we may think forgiveness is either impossible or unnecessary. However, forgiveness is an act done by one and requires no movement from the offender. No matter whether the person is present in this life or the after-life, our hearts will not be free until we forgive them. Forgiving others is something we **always** have the power to do no matter their situation.

In addition to forgiving other people, whether they are here or gone, at some point in our lives, we will need to entertain the idea of forgiving God. This subject can be tricky for some people. What does God *cause* to happen? What does He *allow* to happen? These questions and doubts are as frustrating as they are necessary. Asking these questions is healthy as long as we surrender any expectations of finding answers. The healing is in the questions more than the answers because no answer will ever truly satisfy.

Allow the Holy Spirit to search your heart. Is there anything you have been blaming God for? Are you holding bitterness and anger against Him? It is okay to admit it. We are safe with Him, and He wants us to be honest if we believe He has wounded us in any way. We must be honest with Him and with ourselves before we can forgive Him and find peace.

When we allow ourselves to make a list of everyone whom we need to forgive, there is someone we commonly overlook: ourselves. It never occurs to us we need to forgive ourselves because we think of forgiveness as something we give only to others. Forgiving ourselves comes with much resistance from within. Often, we become so accustomed to feeling the emotion of guilt that we feel like something is missing if it lifts. We end up feeling guilty for not feeling guilty. Sometimes we try to use unforgiveness of ourselves as a method of accountability. We believe holding on to what we've done keeps us in line and prevents us from doing it again. Also, forgiving ourselves is impossible when we are resisting God's forgiveness. Not knowing who we are in Christ will leave us feeling unworthy of forgiveness. If we have been forgiven by God, then refusing to forgive ourselves takes a special kind of pride and arrogance.

Because of who we are in Christ, we have been made partakers in His divine nature (II Peter 1:4). The forgiving nature of Christ is now our nature. We are like Him in our spirit. So as we talk about what it means to forgive others, we must first rest in the truth that **it is** our nature to forgive. It is who we are. Forgiving others comes naturally to our true selves. Just as it is a bird's nature to sing and a lion's nature to roar, it is our nature to release our offenders, setting them and ourselves free.

In Chapter 2, we were given the opportunity to explore our past and uncover the wounds and rejections we've experienced. Every wound or rejection is significant and needs forgiving, not just the obvious ones. Sometimes, the seemingly small hurts can still be very damaging; our soul can experience death by a thousand paper cuts. Take all the offenses committed against you. The wounds. The anger. The bitterness and pain. You cannot be free while you are still clenching that list in your fist. Just as God does not want your own wrongdoings to stand between you and peace, neither does He want someone else's actions to rob you of your peace and freedom. Take it all and nail it to the cross. Then turn your back on it, walk away, and embrace your future.

> IF WE HAVE BEEN FORGIVEN BY GOD, THEN REFUSING TO FORGIVE OURSELVES TAKES A SPECIAL KIND OF PRIDE AND ARROGANCE.

When we forgive those who have hurt us, we are exercising one of the most powerful gifts God has given us. We experience a drastic change in our inner environment and will find ourselves feeling lighter, freer, and more at peace. We become kinder and more loving to those around us. Our hearts fill with gratitude, joy, compassion, and hope. We begin to see the world through the clarity of a new lens. We become more aware of God's presence and can identify ourselves with Him more readily. As our journey continues, forgiveness becomes a lifestyle. Our hearts remain free as our true selves thrive.

May you forgive because it is who you are, and may you live in radical freedom through a lifestyle of forgiveness.

Prayer

*Father, grant me clarity regarding whom I'm holding unforgiveness against. Help me lay my weapons down and with empty hands begin to move toward forgiveness. Remove all barriers standing in the way of the emotional healing I will receive by forgiving. In Your timing, allow my heart to be moved with compassion for those who hurt me. I receive the truth that **it is** my true nature to forgive. From my true self, I want to give others, myself, and even You what You have given me: the gift of forgiveness. Amen.*

In Your Journal...

1. What are some reasons you tend to hold on to unforgiveness?

2. What are you putting at risk by not forgiving yourself, God, and others who have hurt you?

3. How would your life be different if you no longer held on to the hurts and grudges weighing you down?

FURTHER EXERCISES

Forgiving Others

1. Create some sacred space to pray and ask the Holy Spirit to reveal the people who have offended and hurt you. Make a list of all who come to mind. Refer to your journal exercises and/or charts from Chapter 2.

2. Beside each name, write what the person did to offend or hurt you.

3. Write down the lie(s) you believed about yourself as a result of the hurt or offense.

4. Allow yourself to fully feel the hurt, rejection, betrayal, sadness, or any other emotions that arise.

5. Write a letter to each person on your list. Pour your heart out as you tell them what they've done to hurt or offend you and how it has affected your life. The person will never read the letter, so do not concern yourself with their reaction. At the end of the letter, make a confident statement of forgiveness. (Example: "Just as God has forgiven me, I forgive you. I cancel the debt I have been carrying inside. I set you free, and I set myself free.") Read the letter out loud, and make the decision to forgive them. It is often helpful to have someone with you as you read the letter.

6. Pray for the person and wish them well.

7. Destroy the letter (burn, shred, tear up, etc.)

Forgiving Yourself

1. Make a list of all of the things that you know you need to forgive yourself for. It may be helpful to refer back to the list of false self behaviors in Chapter 4.

2. Stand or sit in front of a mirror. Begin by acknowledging the presence of God and His forgiveness. Then read the list out loud to yourself. With each item, ponder how your behavior has affected yourself and others.

3. Look yourself in the eyes and choose to forgive yourself. Make the statement: "Just as God has forgiven me, I choose to forgive myself. I am free."

4. Destroy the list.

Forgiving God

1. Write a letter to God telling Him what you've been holding against Him. Honestly express all your hurts and frustrations with Him.

2. At the end of the letter, forgive God and let Him off the hook. Your statement may sound something like: "Father, today I choose to forgive you, and I release the hurt that I've allowed to hinder our relationship."

3. Destroy the letter.

CHAPTER ELEVEN

JUDGMENTS AND VOWS

A Recipe for Agony

I MAGINE YOU'VE SPENT YOUR ENTIRE LIFE eating nothing but fast food and candy. Your body would still somewhat function, but you would feel sluggish and depressed and be prone to illness. Now imagine you begin to fuel your body with foods God has hand-crafted just for you. You would begin to feel more alive and healthy because your body now has the proper nutrition needed to feel strong. We experience something very similar when we realize we've been allowing judgments and vows to be the food fueling our souls, driving our motives and attitudes. The indwelling life of Christ is the supernatural food our souls need to live a life of freedom and true adventure.

Judging is at the center of many of our problems and can serve as a main ingredient in our recipe for agony. Keep in mind, these judgments can be focused on other people, ourselves, and God. Having our eyes opened to how easily we fall into the trap of judging can set us free from meaningless self-talk and the anger that comes with it.

When we judge, we are trying to control how we feel about ourselves. We will judge ourselves positively if we believe we deserve to feel good; on the flip side, we will judge ourselves negatively when we believe we deserve to feel bad. Even when we judge others and God, we are still indirectly putting the focus on ourselves and how we feel. Our judgments of others come from our own insecurities. As our insecurities lift, our tendency towards judgment will lift as well.

Judgment is not to be confused with discernment, nor with observation. To discern is to recognize, sense, or perceive something, while to observe is to watch and learn. These are beneficial actions designed to lead us to explore, ask questions, and come to healthy conclusions. If we allow discernment and observation to have their proper place, we will become more curious and wise. Unfortunately, fear and insecurity often take our discernment and observation down a painful road into judgment.

While some people may wonder if healthy judgment exists, for the sake of simplicity, when we speak of judgment, we are referring to an attitude of the heart. Sometimes we know when we are being judgmental. We feel it. However, we all have blind spots as well, areas where we're not even aware of being judgmental until someone else calls us on it. Being judgmental can make us feel powerful, right, and justified. Judgment is a condition of the soul, and you are the only one who knows whether you struggle with it. To ask "Am I judging if I say this or do that?" is the wrong approach. The question "Am I judging?" can only be measured by looking inside to our attitudes, not by measuring behavior.

Our judgments are fear-based. Before we judge, a fear must already be in place, which is why we don't automatically judge everyone for everything. If we have no fear concerning a certain type of person or situation, there will be no judgment. Our fears create the filter through which we process our discernments and observations. These pre-existing, fear-based filters create our prejudices (pre-judgments).

For example, if we prejudge ourselves as being weak, we will tend to avoid risks then judge ourselves as weak for avoiding those risks. We will also be more likely to judge others as being weak. The characteristics in others that tend to get under our skin are the same characteristics we fear possessing ourselves.

Jesus tells us to make sure the plank is removed from our own eye before we try to remove the speck from someone else's (Matthew 7:3-5). We tend to focus on what is wrong with others because we have already judged ourselves as being wrong. When our fears and judgment concerning ourselves are removed, we will have clearer vision to see others with grace and compassion instead of judgment.

AS OUR INSECURITIES LIFT, OUR TENDENCY TOWARDS JUDGMENT WILL LIFT AS WELL.

Having a judgmental attitude causes us to become hyper focused on others' behavior as well as our own. Our standards and expectations create an inner environment of performance-based acceptance, and authentic relationships become nearly impossible. We become deeply concerned with how others perform and less interested in them as people who have value regardless of behavior. Over time, having a judgmental attitude creates a critical heart as our true selves become buried under the layers upon layers of our judgmental false self.

Whenever we make a judgment, a cause and effect principle will apply. For every judgment we make, a vow follows on its heels without exception. Vows following judgments are as constant and reliable as thunder following lightning. Some vows are big, bold, and stand out at the forefront of our consciousness, while others are formed in quiet and subtle fashion, staying hidden in our subconscious.

The vows that follow judgments sound something like this:

> *I will never/ I will always*
> *At least I never/ At least I always*
> *At least I am/ At least I am not*

For example, if we judge our father for ruling with an iron fist, the accompanying vow may sound like, "I will never treat my kids that way." Or if we judge our mother for not standing up to our abusive father, the vow may be, "I will always protect my children."

Over time, after we become what we judge (more on that later), our vows can begin to sound like, "I may have yelled at my children, but at least I never hit them" or "I may not have protected my kids from their father, but at least I explained to them why he is abusive."

Making these inner vows such as "I will never" and "I will always" seems like the right thing to do on the surface. We hear tales all the time of a person who experiences something bad then vows to become or do the opposite. Our society tends to celebrate these stories. Vows of this nature may seem noble in the moment but are accompanied by a genuine danger that goes unrealized and ignored. Here is the way it normally works: We make a judgment that comes with a vow, and then we become what we judge. Our goal is to live a life of freedom, treating people with love and respect, not because we've vowed to but **because it's what we want to do.**

In the previous example, we judged our father as angry and controlling then we made a vow never to be like him. Given enough time, we will find ourselves doing the same things we vowed never to do. We become angry and controlling ourselves, possibly even worse than our father, or maybe to a lesser degree ("At least I never"), but angry and controlling all the same. The frustration and confusion of becoming what we judge keeps us locked into unhealthy patterns of living.

A small number of people seem to have the self-discipline to keep the vow and avoid becoming what they judge; however, these people are still not living in freedom. They are bound by their vows. Their judgment is their guide instead of their spirit. Their fear constrains them instead of love releasing them. Their attitudes and behaviors are motivated by their vows instead of by the Holy Spirit.

> JUDGMENTS CAN BE BROKEN AND VOWS CAN BE RENOUNCED THROUGH THE POWER OF THE HOLY SPIRIT.

The trap of judgments and vows can seem inescapable, but there is hope. Judgments can be broken and vows can be renounced through the power of the Holy Spirit. We can live free from the fear and anger that keep the attitude of judging alive within us. We can also experience a new source that motivates us as our vows are renounced and surrendered. Our true selves have no need to judge and find vows to be useless. We see ourselves, others, and God through new eyes, we hear the sounds of the world with new ears, and we discover a new source of life and a new way to live.

May you be marked as counter-cultural because you no longer live in judgment, and may you soar from one adventure to the next, no longer tied to your vows.

PRAYER

Father, I confess I have taken Your gifts of discernment and observation and used them to create judgments. Clearly show me the misery I have created for myself by judging others, myself, and You. I do not wish to rely on my inner vows for motivation any longer. I want to live the way You created me to live, liberated from the bondage of judgments and vows, and free to allow the gifts of Your spirit to guide my steps instead. Amen.

IN YOUR JOURNAL...

---

1. How do you feel when you judge someone?

2. In what ways have you noticed yourself becoming like someone you've judged?

3. When you think about renouncing all of your vows and releasing the influence they have over your life, how do you feel? Why?

Further Exercises

On a sheet of paper (or more than one, if necessary), make two columns. In the left column, write down whom you have judged and what those judgments are. In the right column, write down the vow that came with each judgment. Follow the example below:

JUDGMENT	VOW
I judged Dad for ruling with an iron fist	I vowed never to raise my kids that way
I judged Dad for cheating on Mom	I vowed never to cheat on my wife
I judged Mom for being passive	I vowed never to be passive
I judged Mom for gossiping	I vowed never to gossip
I judged my pastor for lying to our church	I vowed always to be honest
I judged myself for screaming at my kids	I vowed never to scream at them again
I judged my wife for trying to control me	I vowed never to try to control her
I judged God for allowing tragedy in my life	I vowed to prevent tragedy from happening to those I love

Referring to your list, break each judgment and renounce its associated vow out loud. You might use this prayer as an example: "Father, I break my judgment of Dad for ruling with an iron fist, and I renounce my vow, 'I will never raise my kids that way'." Once you have broken every judgment and renounced every vow, destroy the list. Afterwards, ask the Holy Spirit to show you when you make future judgments and when you are being motivated by a new vow instead of by His love.

CHAPTER TWELVE

GRIEVING

Both Human and Divine

WE HAVE ALL EXPERIENCED LOSSES, whether large or small, obvious or subtle, tangible or intangible. Our false self's response to a loss is to turn away from it; however, we have been divinely designed for something else. We have been made to turn into the pain of a loss, not away from it. To grieve is both human and divine. Whether a loss is large or small, grieving well is the only response that keeps our hearts free to feel the fullness of life and our minds unencumbered to have peace in the present.

We grieve because we were made in the image of God, and we are His family. Even Jesus Himself experienced grief. He had a special relationship with Lazarus and his sisters, and when Lazarus died, Jesus joined the sisters and they all grieved together (John 11:33-35). When Jesus became aware of the death of His cousin, John the Baptist, He withdrew to a solitary place because He needed to be alone with the news for a while (Matthew 14:13). Even though Jesus knew death would not have the final word for Lazarus or John the Baptist, He did not allow that truth to prevent Him from grieving. If Jesus needed to grieve in order to live fully alive then so do we.

While it may be tempting to believe we need to grieve only the largest or most obvious losses, the truth is that we need to grieve them all. One minor, ungrieved loss on its own may not have a huge impact on our souls; however, as the smaller losses begin to stack up, their accumulation can cause us to feel weighed down.

Just as we must grieve our losses, acknowledging and lingering in the celebrations of life is an important part of feeling all the emotions we were designed to feel. Opportunities for celebrating are much more common than we realize. When we learn how to slow down and soak in the opportunities for enjoyment, even the smallest of celebrations can help keep us focused on what is good. By falling into a pattern of simply brushing past opportunities to celebrate, we run the risk of becoming numb, and the power of gratitude will have no positive impact on our lives.

If we want to experience the fullness of joy that comes from being a divinely created human being, we must celebrate every gain, no matter how large or small. And if we want to experience peace in the present with no weights from the past, we must learn to grieve every loss. To celebrate every gain and grieve every loss is to wake up from apathy and live fully alive.

Losses we need to grieve can take many forms. Some of the more obvious ones include death, divorce, the end of a relationship or friendship, abortion, miscarriage, infidelity, and being the victim of or witnessing abuse. Other events needing to be grieved can be harder to recognize, including the loss of a job, physical impairments, loss of parts of childhood, or loss of a dream. Sometimes, as our concept of self begins to change and heal, we may even need to grieve the loss of the false selves we shed along the way. Letting go of something that has hurt us is still a loss, and we may need to grieve even if what we've lost was not good for us and we are better off without it.

As we experience a loss, we are faced with multiple factors. We are not only feeling the void that the loss created, but also struggling with the beliefs the loss has imprinted on our souls. These beliefs can affect how we view ourselves, our relationships, and our future. They often take the form of "I" statements: I will never be happy again. I will never get past this. I am damaged forever. I will never get close enough to experience a loss again. I deserved this. I am being punished.

From these distorted beliefs, new aspects of our false selves are created or existing aspects are validated. When we are not resting and abiding in who we truly are, these false beliefs begin to shape our lives. We may begin to avoid or sabotage opportunities for happiness. We stall out in the process instead of continuing through it. In short, all our beliefs become a self-fulfilling prophecy—we will create what we believe. By attempting to grieve from the false self, we run the risk of getting completely lost in the chaotic self-talk accompanying our distorted beliefs.

> TO CELEBRATE EVERY GAIN AND GRIEVE EVERY LOSS IS TO WAKE UP FROM APATHY AND LIVE FULLY ALIVE.

However, when we know who we are and grieve from our true selves, our suffering is infused with intimacy, and we know even the dark night of the soul holds a divine purpose. And when we know who God truly is, we are reminded in the midst of our suffering that He is for us, He is with us, and He is connected to us with compassion.

When our false beliefs and false selves take over the grieving process, we can experience a range of unhealthy responses to a loss rather than truly grieving it. Although grieving is mostly painful, it is a therapeutic need of the soul. In our efforts to avoid or control our grieving process, we might replace what we lost, trying to fill the hole it has left inside us so we don't have to acknowledge what we're missing. Even if we don't deliberately attempt to replace it, we might try to avoid thinking about our loss by throwing ourselves into work, family, or other areas of our lives that can keep us busy. We can even try to replace the loss with religion, immersing ourselves in church activities. This can have the appearance of positivity and moving forward, but any activities, even religious ones, can be unhealthy if they keep a person from feeling the emotions they need to feel in the moment.

ALTHOUGH GRIEVING IS MOSTLY PAINFUL, IT IS A THERAPEUTIC NEED OF THE SOUL.

Avoiding anything that reminds us of the loss is also very common. For example, if someone is fired from a job they love, they may hesitate to seek another job in the same field in order to avoid being reminded of the loss, even though that particular field may be their calling. Another way of avoiding thinking about the loss, and avoiding the emotions accompanying those thoughts, is to self-medicate with drugs, alcohol, pornography, food, or shopping. Regardless of how we choose to avoid dealing with our losses, we can only ignore and numb our emotions for so long before they begin to leak out in ways we can't control.

While some of us may choose to replace what we have lost or do whatever we can to avoid thinking about it, others dive headlong into an identity of victimhood. We may become stuck in a particular emotion of grief, such as anger, guilt, or depression, to the exclusion of all other emotions, until we become confused about who we are and turn our loss into our sole identity.

After an especially enormous loss, such as the death of a spouse or child, the grieving process for some people might take years, and the wounds may always be tender. What constitutes healthy grieving has no set timeline, and it can be difficult to know whether we are grieving slowly, but healthily, or are stuck in the process and need help moving forward. However, the grieving process is called a process for a reason. The name itself implies some sort of continuous movement or change, however slow. Becoming stuck in place and staying there indefinitely is not a process and is not healthy.

What role does time play in the grieving process? If you are mistaken about time's role, looking to time as a component of healing will do more damage than good. One of the most tragic misconceptions the soul deals with is the belief that time heals all wounds. If we place our trust and attention into the passage of time to bring healing, the loss gets buried deep inside our souls, creating confusion. From time to time, we experience the loss attempting to crawl out of the grave time buried it in. We've assumed the pain of the loss is dead when in truth it's right under the surface.

Time does play a part in the grieving process if we allow our wounds to remain open for healing. If not, the only thing time does to our wounds is allow them to become infected. Imagine suffering a deep cut on your arm. Instead of going through the necessary steps to allow your wound to heal properly, you simply cover the cut and try to forget about it. After time, the wound may appear healed on the surface, but just below the surface, infection has set in. At this point, a doctor may have to reopen the wound, exposing and cleaning it so you can heal from the inside out.

Wounds in the soul created by losses can work the same way sometimes. We need our wounds reopened and our losses revisited. After this point, time can become a component of healing, because it *is* necessary. But now God is using time as an instrument of healing, rather than our false selves using time as an instrument of burying, forgetting, and infecting.

Some experts have divided the grieving process into a variety of stages people pass through while journeying from the initial moment of loss to some sort of resolution. Understanding these stages, often divided into denial, anger, bargaining, depression, and acceptance, can be helpful for putting names to some very confusing feelings. Additionally, understanding that these feelings are normal and may take many months or even years to work through can be helpful in the face of outside pressure to "just get over it and move on."

Unfortunately, for some people, the word "stages" can be misleading. They hear the term and assume each stage is a completely separate category of feeling, distinct from other stages, and that by working through a checklist, a person can mark off each stage and be done with grief.

The reality is that grieving is rarely, if ever, so neat and clean. It is much more common for a person to feel many emotions at once. And often, people may find themselves looping back on an emotion they thought they were done with. "I thought I was finished with anger," a grieving spouse might say, "but then I found our wedding album and I was angry all over again." In this manner, thinking of the emotions and mindsets of grief as stages can do more harm than good, because the grieving person (or their friends and family) may view revisiting a previous emotion as lack of progress or even regression. Realistically, what they're feeling is an entirely appropriate response.

Every person may not experience every stage of grief for the same length of time. Some people may skip a stage entirely. Others may pass through some stages quickly then find themselves lingering in one. This does not mean they are not grieving "properly." It just means the grieving process is very complicated and is different for each person. Even if two people have experienced the same loss, grief will be manifested differently in each of their lives.

Because thinking of grief as a series of stages can be misleading, it may be more accurate to think of the grieving process as a variety of emotions a person may experience. The most common emotions surrounding grief are shock or denial, anger, bargaining, sadness and depression, guilt, acceptance, and resolution. These can happen in any order. A person can certainly be feeling more than one emotion at the same time, and they may have to pass through a particular emotion more than once.

The emotions of grieving can be so loud that we will definitely have days when God seems silent. When grieving from our false selves, we can easily interpret the silence as abandonment and attempt to fill it ourselves with whatever we can. Grieving from our true selves, though, allows us to recognize that God's silence does not equal His absence. His silence has a purpose. God sits quietly with us in our grief, and oftentimes silence is more sacred than words. In these moments, the silence of God can fill us and become the most loving expression of Himself He can give.

If you stopped the grieving process too early or never started to begin with, if false beliefs and false selves have distorted your grieving process, you will need to go backward before you can go forward. It is important to grieve all losses you have not fully grieved. This may take some time, but start sooner rather than later. It's time to get caught up. Empty your emotional tank by feeling all the emotions you have stored up that never had their day. You must start in the past and grieve your way forward to catch up with the peace waiting for you in the present moment.

GOD'S SILENCE DOES NOT EQUAL HIS ABSENCE.

As you begin to learn what healthy grieving feels like, you may find yourself wondering whether the grieving process has a specific end point. Some people will tell you they know exactly when they were finished grieving a particular loss. Others may say they never really finished; they simply reached a place where grief was no longer at the forefront of their hearts and minds. The reason there are so many opinions on when and if grief ends is that every person and every situation is different. However, there must be a progression forward. We walk *through* the valley of the shadow of death (Psalm 23:4). We don't want to sprint through it nor sit down in it.

In the initial season of the grieving process, the emotions we feel may be stronger than the presence of hope. However, even if we only have a sliver of hope, that sliver is all we need to move forward. As we move forward, hope grows and the grief lessens until hope is at the forefront of our minds and occupies a majority of our hearts.

What does healthy grieving look like in our future? After we get caught up on the ungrieved losses from our past, we then want to adopt a posture of grieving losses in real time as they happen. We allow ourselves to fully feel what the loss brings in the present moment. We remain connected to what is real and what is happening inside us. No longer stunting our growth by storing emotions, we move forward and experience the sacredness of grieving.

May you come to know the humanity and divinity of celebrating every gain and grieving every loss, and may both teach you to live fully alive.

PRAYER

Father, You have designed me to experience gains and losses as You do. Your love gives me the courage to patiently face significant events I rushed through or ignored altogether. I give you permission to wake me up emotionally. Teach me, Father, to live fully alive. Amen.

IN YOUR JOURNAL...

1. Explain why it may be difficult to accept grieving as a part of God's nature and therefore as part of yours.

2. What have been some of your unhealthy responses to loss in the past?

3. Why is learning how to properly grieve important for living fully alive?

Further Exercises

1. Make a list of the losses you have experienced ranging from most to least significant. A loss can refer to a person, a physical thing such as a house, or an intangible thing such as a job or your childhood. Even if something or someone was not good for you, grieving the loss may still be a necessary part of your healing. Remember, grieving your way through the past in order to catch up to the present may take time.

2. Start with the top three losses on your list. For each of these three people or things, write a letter in which you express what they meant to you, whether good or bad or some combination of both. Then write about how you have honestly felt since the loss occurred. Spend some time considering the person or thing's significance and how the loss has impacted your life, allowing yourself to fully feel the weight of this loss. At the end of each of your three letters, say goodbye.

3. Complete a symbolic act with each of your letters. For example, you might read the letter aloud to a friend, mentor, or counselor. If the letter is to a person who is deceased, then if at all possible visit the person's grave and read the letter aloud to them. You might also consider having a personal funeral of your own and burying the letter.

4. When you feel you are ready, go to the next three items on your list and repeat these steps.

Chapter Thirteen

SURRENDER

Where Love and Fear Collide

SURRENDERING OUR ENTIRE LIVES to God is frequently misunderstood. Most people picture a battlefield scene in which one side is beaten into submission by the other and has no choice but to give up. Bloody and battered, they finally wave a white flag and submit themselves to whatever penalties the victors choose to impose. However, truly surrendering to God brings freedom rather than defeat.

Surrender is not a resignation; it is a relinquishment. It is not giving up; it is giving to. It is not passive; it is passionate. It is not waving a white flag in defeat; it is basking under the banner of God's love.

Even though surrender is difficult to define, once we get a taste of surrendered life, we know when we are surrendered and when we are not. We sense it. We feel it in our bodies. We know when we are carrying the weight that comes with our attempts to control, and we know when the weight lifts. At this point in your journey, you may never have tasted the freedom of surrender. The weight might feel normal. If so, here is something of a warning: Should you choose to explore what a recklessly abandoned soul feels like, you will be ruined to what most consider a "normal" life.

As we consider what we need to surrender, it is easier to identify the people and things that are clearly harmful to us, such as toxic relationships, addictions, greed, dishonesty, and obsessions. However, what about the things and people God has given to us? The word surrender comes from the Latin *redere*, which means "to give back." There come seasons in our lives when God calls on us to give back what He has given to us: hopes, dreams, talents, gifts, intellect, circumstances, careers, possessions, money, and loved ones past and present. God is not asking for these things back because He no longer wants us to have them. He simply wants us to share them with Him and release control.

> SURRENDER IS NOT A RESIGNATION; IT IS A RELINQUISHMENT.

Surrender affects the entirety of our lives. Imagine yourself standing before God, your hands extended in front of you and your life resting on your upturned palms. Surrender is trusting God enough to allow your hands to remain open. It is not a move toward passivity, or a lack of interest or engagement. You have dreams, desires, and goals, but they are held in your open hands, without trying to control them. Control happens when we close our hands and attempt to white-knuckle our way through our days.

Below is a list of common things we attempt to control. You may need to surrender your right to:

Possessions

Prosper financially

Be accepted by others

Pleasant circumstances

A healthy, attractive body

Strength of mind, emotions, and will

Take offense

Be right

Plan your future

A mate, home, or children

A happy marriage or family

Choose your recreation/ entertainment

Be loved

Have visible security

Be used of God

A positive work environment

Promotions and career advancement

A good reputation

Be successful

Know the will of God

Friendships

Be heard

Avoid reaping what you sow

See results

Live where you want to live

Protect your habits

Defy authority

Life itself

We must recognize each individual person or thing in need of surrendering; however, we can simplify the way we think about this process. The surrendering of our souls encompasses not only the people and things we need to surrender, but also what they represent to us.

Imagine again that you stand before God, hands extended, palms up. Instead of opening our hands from around the people and things we've been clutching, we are now presenting our entire selves to Him, even our minds. Our normal thought processes are in dire need of transformation because so much of our focus is on controlling the people and things around us in order to feel safe, secure, and satisfied. But as we've previously discussed, all these attempts at control leave us feeling exhausted and empty. What if our thoughts stopped leading us to acts of control and began nurturing attitudes of surrender? Allowing the Holy Spirit to guide our thought processes is the crux of living a free life.

WHATEVER WE FIXATE ON MENTALLY IS WHAT WILL CONTROL US EMOTIONALLY.

In addition to our thought processes, we also need to surrender the associated emotions. We are prone to allowing our emotional state to dictate so much of our lives. Many of our choices are made because we desire to feel or not feel certain emotions; we're either trying to create a particular emotional state or avoid it altogether. Within this desire is where our most obsessive, controlling patterns are found. Whatever we fixate on mentally is what will control us emotionally, regardless of whether these are emotions we're trying to chase or run away from.

Everything in our lives is centered on our emotions, including our hopes, desires, goals, and dreams. Even our most basic daily activities are driven by chasing certain emotional states and avoiding others. For example, we work to make money to pay our bills in order to meet our basic needs and wants, so we can **feel** more secure and less stressed.

Even the way we relate to the people around us, our parents, children, bosses, co-workers, and friends, can be centered on minimizing our stress and maximizing other feelings such as accomplishment, security, and love.

One of the riskiest prayers we can pray concerns our emotional life. Take a minute and become familiar with the following. Then when you are willing to take the risk, actually give your emotional life over to God using this prayer:

> *"Father, I surrender my emotional life to you. I open myself up to feel every emotion, whether pleasant or unpleasant, that I need to feel in order to live fully alive. I also surrender my right to feel the emotions you know I am prone to chase. I trust you. Amen."*

Along with our thoughts and emotions, our will must be surrendered as well. An unsurrendered will is easy to detect through its unmistakable attitude, such as, "I want what I want, when I want it, and how I want it." It is absorbed with the false self and centered on its own interest. Other times, a will is unsurrendered because we've allowed fear or shame to cripple it. An unsurrendered will can lead to nothing but conflict and frustration and will bring death to peace, joy, integrity, and meaningful relationships. As we begin to open our hands and allow God to have a place in our decisions, we will find our focus, interests, and passions to be placed in a direction bringing life, peace, and true adventure.

When we think about what we need to surrender and why, many hindrances can keep us from following through. Often, we confuse the *decision* to surrender with the *act* of surrender. Imagine ten birds on a wire. If five of them decide to fly away, how many are left? Most people will say five, but the answer is really ten because making a decision is not the same as following through on it. The decision needs to be accompanied by a gesture of surrender, a symbolic act to help you mark the beginning of your path, but you must remember the act is only the first step in a lifestyle of surrender.

Just as the decision to surrender should not be mistaken for the act of following through, neither should we confuse knowledge of the process for actually going through it. Sometimes, learning about surrender can make us feel like we have already gone through the process, when in reality we have just begun. We also may be unwilling to surrender because we are unwilling to give up control, even if control is an illusion. Perhaps we are afraid of the unknown. Sometimes our pride prevents us from surrendering. Other times, it is our unwillingness to suffer. Many of us have held on to secrets from our pasts that keep us locked inside our own heads, unable to break free. We may have fooled ourselves into believing we don't really need to surrender because we think the mediocre lives we're now leading are good enough. And some of us refuse to surrender because we are in open rebellion toward God.

However, the biggest reason why many of us don't surrender is that we still have a distorted view of God's character. Why would we give the most fragile or most important parts of ourselves to a God we don't trust?

Asking ourselves if we trust God is an important question. However, the question gains even more power when it is asked by God Himself. To a certain extent, we are programmed to ask God questions and wait for His answers. Not only is this a common form of prayer; it is also a common way of relating to others. Questions create a dialog, and dialog leads to a relationship. In the New Testament, we find Jesus continually asking questions of the people around Him. He is not merely preaching to them and telling parables. He knows asking questions and listening to people's answers is one of the strongest ways to build relationships.

We ask questions of God. But how much deeper could our relationship with God grow if we took the time to ask Him, "What questions do you have for me?" Once we wade through everything we imagine God might ask about our specific choices and situations, most of us will find the main question He has for us is this: "Do you trust me?" Trust is the backbone of surrender. We will not trust someone whom we do not believe loves us, likes us, and is for us.

> WE MAY HAVE FOOLED OURSELVES INTO BELIEVING WE DON'T REALLY NEED TO SURRENDER BECAUSE WE THINK THE MEDIOCRE LIVES WE'RE NOW LEADING ARE GOOD ENOUGH.

Allow your life to be a process of discovering God passionately loves you, intimately likes you, and is unwaveringly for you. You can trust Him and enjoy a shared life with the One who knows you best. You don't have to live with the fear and pressure that come from control. It's okay to open up your clenched fists and allow blood to flow freely into your fingers, where before it was cut off. Similarly, you can open your soul and allow life to flow freely into areas where your attempts to control previously kept peace at bay.

Begin now. Don't wait. Let this be the season when you experience the pathway to peace through surrender. Surrender is a lifelong process beginning with a single decision. Sooner rather than later, decide. Decide to share your life. Decide to open your hands.

Surrender gives us the opportunity to experience the present moment and the peace found there. While reflecting on the past can be beneficial, having a head full of chatter about the past is torture. Likewise, planning and dreaming about the future have their place, but when our minds feel like a constantly running motor, anxiety is the result. Mentally relinquishing both directions, the past and the future, is a practice developed over time. Surrender is a key component of this art.

> SURRENDER IS NOT PASSIVE. IN FACT, IT IS THE BRAVEST AND MOST PRODUCTIVE THING YOU WILL EVER DO.

When we surrender and turn inside to that place where we're joined with God, we discover what it means to experience the Eternal here and now. Peace lives in that sacred space known as the present moment, and there we find His life and a place to rest. While resting, we are able to see, hear, smell, touch, and even taste the riches found in Philippians 4:8. We find the truth that leads to freedom, the honor and justice that allow us to raise our chins, and the pure beauty of the gift of life. Surrender is the pathway, and while the details will vary, the essence of surrender is timeless and transcends circumstances.

Unfortunately, our natural reaction to most situations is motivated by the mindset of the false self. We are set in our ways and easily develop dysfunctional rhythms. When we feel uncomfortable or out of control, we may be quick to judge, attempt to take control, manipulate the situation to gain a desired outcome, or talk ourselves into or out of discomfort. We might also worry or obsess over the situation or hide in passivity. The saddest part about living this way is that it feels normal until we experience something different.

Brokenness and surrender allow us to experience something unique and special. Surrender from an attitude of brokenness transcends the pressure of trying to modify our behavior, freeing us to experience a different life source altogether so our true selves may live, thrive, and flourish.

When we attempt to control from our false selves, we create conflict and frustration, no matter how good our intentions. However, when we surrender, we live from an endless reservoir of the fruits of the Spirit, which are love, joy, peace, patience, kindness, goodness, faithfulness, gentleness, and self-control (Galatians 5:22-23). Surrender is not passive. In fact, it is the bravest and most productive thing you will ever do.

One of the most difficult parts of our false self to allow to be broken is the part that self-protects. It's one thing to guard our hearts with an attitude of discernment and wisdom, but it is another thing entirely to never open up and be vulnerable enough to risk being hurt. A surrendered heart is one willing to risk being fully known and face the possibility of rejection. Not only do we often protect ourselves from possible rejection, as strange as it may seem, we also sometimes resist and push away love. The reasons vary. Some of us may feel unworthy of love. Others push love away because we intuitively know that along with it comes the possibility of pain. For some, love equals weakness. Others of us have never been able to trust anyone enough to allow ourselves to receive love.

Surrender is a lifestyle, a continual emptying of our fears, rights, entitlements, and selfishness. We reach a place of surrender by allowing God's love to carry us there, and we leave it by listening to the voice of fear telling us God is not as loving and trustworthy as we need Him to be. Surrender takes vulnerability and embracing the reality that we're fully known, that God sees through all our masks and facades. We are naked before Him. The question is, are we afraid? Are we ashamed? Surrender. Fall into His love. He promises to never leave us and to always love us.

May you be released from the fear that tempts you to control, and may God's love draw you to the peace of surrender.

Prayer

Father, I cannot surrender if I do not trust You. Nothing I attempt to control can flourish, and trying to keep such a strong grip on myself and others will leave me exhausted. Please show me every area of my life where I am lacking trust, and flood me with love until I unclench my grip and open my hands. Gently lead me into surrender so I can find what my soul has always longed for—peace. Amen.

In Your Journal...

1. Describe the difference between the "white flag" form of surrender and the surrender described in this chapter.

2. Describe the chatter in your head that makes surrender difficult for you.

3. Trust is essential to surrender. In what areas of your life do you struggle to trust God?

4. What is the worst thing that can happen if you surrender? What is the best?

Further Exercise

We can identify what or whom we need to surrender by asking ourselves several questions. What are my fears? What or whom do I feel entitled to have? Whom or what am I trying to control?

Buy a helium filled balloon. With a felt-tipped marker, write on the balloon all your fears, all your entitlement, and everyone and everything you are tempted to try to control.

Find a quiet place outdoors and release the balloon to God as a symbolic step of your commitment to a lifestyle of surrender.

CONCLUSION
So May You...

REGARDLESS OF WHERE YOU ARE on your journey, the essentials found in this book can enrich your life beyond measure. Countless people have found peace and freedom by cooperating with the Holy Spirit and having the courage to be intentional about their healing and growth. This process is not a "one and done" experience. It is a lifestyle of refining our souls. God is aware that if we tried to deal with all our past, present, and future issues at once, we would implode.

Therefore, be open to revisiting this book from time to time. God knows when we need a season during which not much seems to be happening inside us, and He knows when the time is right for us to dive back into another round of healing. He is the Wonderful Counselor who has the wisdom to perfectly lead us down the path of healing, growth, and rest. God loves us just the way we are, yet He loves us far too much to leave us the way we are. Knowing this will keep us intimately connected to Him no matter what season of life we are in.

Sometimes we experience healing that seems maintenance-free, when a lie we have believed seems to instantly disappear into the abyss, never to return. Other times, a lie may linger even after it has been exposed and revelation has been received. For example, one of the most common lies we can believe centers on our value. One person may have believed the lie that they were worthless, but after receiving the revelation of who they are in Christ, they never struggled with that belief again. On the other hand, another person could believe the same lie and receive the same revelation, and on occasion still struggle with feeling worthless.

This is when setting the mind becomes of the utmost importance. If we do not choose what we focus on, our minds will automatically set themselves based on how we are programmed. We are invited into a sacred mindset that results in peace, and this path is laid out for us in Philippians 4:8-9, when Paul writes, "Whatever is true, whatever is honorable, whatever is just, whatever is pure, whatever is lovely, whatever is commendable, if there is any excellence, if there

MAY THE WATERS
AROUND YOU
NEVER BE CALM
AGAIN.

is anything worthy of praise, think about these things." The greatest benefit in setting our mind comes when we do it in the form of conversations with God. Rehearsing truth in our minds over and over is one thing. Exchanging these truths back and forth with the One who is Truth is altogether different. Our relationship with God is the foundation a life of peace is built on, and no relationship can thrive without communication.

While our relationship with God is the most important part of our lives, God did not design us to be islands; rather, He made us to connect with others as well as Himself. Even if we are unaware of it, we long for a group of people to know us, to be honest and vulnerable with.

As a part of a group, you will give as well as receive, which is what makes it so rewarding. However, along with a group, you will greatly benefit from a few relationships in which you are only on the receiving end. Counselors, coaches, mentors, advisors—these are people you can turn to when you need time solely about you. We all need these outlets, someone completely objective who can speak into our lives in a way someone we are too close with may not. They are there for us and only us. You are worth seeking this out for yourself.

We crave healthy and meaningful relationships because we are created in God's image, and to deny that part of ourselves is to deny who we truly are. We find this characteristic of God when we think about the Trinity, God the Father, Son, and Holy Spirit living and functioning in relationship with each other. We are made for relationship because at our core, we find a relational God.

God has gifted us with many avenues to strengthen our awareness of our connection with Him. He is neither inside nor outside the box. With God, there is no box. Allow your spiritual antennae to rise and receive the Holy Spirit's signals, leading you to explore ways, whether common or uncommon, of heightening your awareness.

Journal, pray, read, write, worship, meditate, teach, learn, sing, dance, draw, paint, serve.

Do these at home, church, coffee shops, in cities, suburbs, in the country side, on the mountain top, at the beach. Do these alone and with others. Discovering your unique way of living in rhythm with the Holy Spirit is enjoyable after the pressure of feeling like you need to perform for God is lifted. Expand your mind and open your heart as you find your flow.

Continually taste and see that the Lord is good (Psalm 34:8) and allow your appetite to grow with every bite. Make healing and growing so much a part of your fabric you can't imagine life without them. As you continue to heal and grow, others will be drawn to you. People have a built-in radar that detects an awakened soul. They sense it and are allured by it. Don't be afraid to help others who are drawn to you. Use this book as a tool to lead them where you have been led.

We stand together in need of healing and growth. We are a society made up of individuals. When we as individuals are liberated from what binds us, we are free to love each other more. As we love each other more, powerful things happen. The ripples from one changed life have the power to rock many boats. May the waters around you never be calm again.

Our Prayer for You Is This:

May you welcome your God-given need for love, and may that need guide you to its Source.

May you become intimately connected with your past, and may you hold it close without letting it hold you back.

May you experience the freedom of putting expectations to rest, and may grace awaken the true desires of your heart.

May you allow your false self to be drawn out from the shadows, and may you receive the truth that your false self is not the real you.

May you allow the beauty of brokenness to have its way with you, and may you experience the joy of living from the inside out.

May you continually search for the truth of who God is, and may the lies you believe about Him be exposed so you can boldly proclaim, "That is not who my God is."

May you truly know Him, and may you stand in the light of His love and proclaim, "This is who my God is."

May you claim your verdict of innocence as you rest in God's sacrificial love, and may you walk in the victory of a resurrected life.

May you experience your true self as you see your reflection in the eyes of your Creator, and may you rest in knowing that you already are all you have been striving to become.

May you forgive because it is who you are, and may you live in radical freedom through a lifestyle of forgiveness.

May you be marked as counter-cultural because you no longer live in judgment, and may you soar from one adventure to the next, no longer tied to your vows.

May you come to know the humanity and divinity of celebrating every gain and grieving every loss, and may both teach you to live fully alive.

May you be released from the fear that tempts you to control, and may God's love draw you to the peace of surrender.

May you live a life of peace and intimacy with God, yourself, and others.

And let it be so...

In Your Journal...

1. What are your thoughts and feelings around the idea healing is not a "one and done" experience but a lifetime of returning to different areas?

2. Does being fully known and vulnerable with others frighten you? Why or why not?

3. Relationships cannot exist without communication. What is preventing you from deepening your communication with God?

Acknowledgments

Special thanks to the following people for their assistance in shaping this book:

Preliminary Think Tank: Dee Ann Whitenton, Bekki Dinsmore, Lizzie Rowan, Ken Pallone

Refining Group: Tamela Mitchell, Tom Boisclair, Tracy Atfield, Anita Dickson, Eric Abney, Marianna Dollyhigh, Melissa Hackney, Michelle Richardson

And a very special thanks to Editor Extraordinaire Laura B. Woznick, the birthing coach who helped bring this book into the world.